Praise For

WHO'S IN CHARGE AROUND HERE?

"Dr. Saffici has done a great job of simplifying the basic guidelines for living a more successful, proactive life. Suitable for people in all walks of life regardless of age. I highly recommend it"
Dr. Bobbe Sommer, Co-author of *Psycho-Cybernetics 2000*

"Chris Saffici distills a lifetime of passionate learning into a clear, inspiring and fun guide to take charge as the CEO of your own life! This is a book that will help you discover exactly who you really are, and to become a shining example of character, success, and self-esteem. Don't just read this book, LIVE IT!"
Brian Biro, author of *Beyond Success* and *Through the Eyes of a Coach*

"Unpretentious ... Dr. Saffici epitomizes a "back to basics" instructional self-help handbook that "zeros-in" on true tested, timeless principles, utilizing a common sense application. Truly influential"
Rocco Boulay, President, Integrity Health Enhancement for Women

"Excellent! This is an easy and insightful read. As my friend Chris Saffici says, "Take the time to make a difference in yourself." I did"
K. C. Keeler, Head Football Coach, University of Delaware, 2003 1AA champions

"An easy to understand and practical guide to a more meaningful life! It is sound in principle, up to date, and personal."
Dr. Kevin Freiberg, Co-author of *GUTS! Companies That Blow the Doors Off Business–as-Usual* and bestseller, *NUTS! Southwest Airlines' Crazy Recipes for Business and Personal Success*

"This book is an invaluable aid to organizational and management skills. Chris has a plan for increasing efficiency and productivity, essentials in my profession"
Larry Kehres, Head Football Coach, Mount Union College, 8 time NCAA Div. III National champions

"Must reading for top athletes and others trying to be their best!"
Angelo Borzio, Head Wrestling Coach East Stroudsburg University

Acknowledgments

With special thanks to:

My wonderful wife, Kristin, and my children Alexa and Ryan. Thank you all for your constant support and understanding as this book was being written.

Ed and Pat at Franklin Publishers who worked tirelessly with me, teaching me the "ins and outs."

Ellen Smith for being such an outstanding editor and for "reengineering" my rough manuscript.

Rodney Dick for being such a thorough proofreader and a wonderful person to work with.

Jeremy Ervin who worked tirelessly with the structure and design.

Angelo Borzio who helped renovate space in my house and declared that a book would be written there.

Warren Wagner who challenged my concepts and helped me solidify the book's structure.

Deidre Ditze who lent her counseling background and female touch to my ideas.

To my support network of Jan Wendt, Jack Truschel, and Scott Piper.

The numerous people who generously shared their ideas and experiences with me.

For everyone I mentioned, there are dozens more whom space does not permit me to name, for which I ask their indulgence.

Christopher Saffici

Who's in Charge Around Here?

Taking Control of Your Life And Making Positive Changes

Christopher L. Saffici, Ed. D.

FRANKLIN PUBLISHERS
PO Box 4915
Pittsburgh, PA 15206

Dedications

To God, who makes my life possible.
May I always strive to be my best
and make a difference in this world.

To Edward Krimmel, a fine man,
a tremendous support in good times
and bad, and a never ending source
of optimism, intelligence and
common sense.

Library of Congress Card No. 2006931616

ISBN 0-916503-09-7
       978-0-916503-09-3   Printed in the Unites States of America

Contents

Introduction

One of the exercises that I have asked my freshman students to do over the years is to write on an index card what they want to do with their lives. On the other side of the card, they answer the question, "If you could do anything you wanted and would not fail, what would that be?" Then I ask them if the answer on both sides of the card is the same and, if not, why? The answers vary, but the truth is that most are afraid to go for the brass ring. Some do not know what they want or really don't dare to go for it, for a variety of reasons. "In a world where mediocrity is the mode, there is no greater challenge than giving your best in whatever you do," Roger Neilson, former NHL coach has said. As a society, we are encouraged to be conservative and are discouraged to think outside of the box. We are not born with these preconceived notions but become conditioned to limit our expectations.

Because success is defined individually, perhaps the only true way to judge success is by how we want to feel inside. If what you do and who you are makes you feel good, then you are successful. Ultimately, success is not measured by what we have or don't have. We can be wealthy and happy or wealthy and miserable; we can be poor and happy or poor and miserable. Simply put, success is determined by how we feel about life, and how we feel about life is determined by what our lives are about.

The happiest and most successful people are those who get things done, get on with their lives, and realize that life is an endless series of choices. They take responsibility for these choices as well as for the consequences of their actions. Successful people choose to control their destiny so that fate and others don't. They believe that choice more than chance determines their circumstances. Even in circumstances for which they are not entirely responsible, they still take responsibility for their actions.

Our past is important, but not nearly as important as our present and our future. Who we were is not who we will have to be. *We do not have to know the way to know there is a way.* Believe in yourself. Persistence has no time limit. We can become just about whatever we want, if we want it badly enough. Our mind will seek validation for our beliefs. Make your beliefs work for you. Our greatest asset is the ability to choose the way we think, act and feel. We all have free will when we choose to exert it. If we do not, other people, other circumstances, and even our own limiting thoughts take over.

The exciting part is that we already have all the tools necessary to change at any time. How unstoppable would we be if we refused to accept the word "no?" If we didn't take a "no" as a personal attack and instead kept modifying our approach, we would be formidable. There is virtually nothing that could stop us.

Be different from the pack; stand out as someone different. Care more than others do. Risk and dream more than others think is possible. Expect more than others think is possible. In doing these things, we set ourselves apart and use more of our potential. In fact, successful people are usually considered outsiders because they are acknowledged as doing things differently than the rest. You can learn anything you need to learn and achieve any goal you want by finding out what others before you have done to get the results they wanted.

The ideas contained in this book will save you years of hard work in achieving the success that you imagine for yourself. This book is a culmination of simple timeless fundamentals that can help you take more control of your life and give you the skills to find success. While conducting research for this book, I was continually reminded that the fundamentals are simple; following them is the difficult part. I was also reminded of the fact that most wisdom is simple; most of the fundamentals are centuries old, yet every generation discovers them anew. The interpretations may vary, or the way they are presented may change, but the premises are consistent and do not change over time. The

Ten Commandments, for example, work because they are easy to understand. Notice that I did not say that they are easy to follow. They are, however, easily understood.

We do not have to reinvent the wheel. We are not talking about "new truth" but, rather, the same principles that others have used to achieve the success they wanted. If others have done it, why can't you? The answer is - you can!

When I began teaching in the public school system, I had many rules for the students to follow, one for just about any possible situation. After a few years of experience, I eliminated many rules and made those that remained more concise. One that remained was: "All students will respect themselves, others, and property." This simplified rule covered just about every problem that could arise on a given day, it became much easier for the children to know the rules and for me to enforce them. However, just because it was simple and understandable didn't mean the rules weren't broken and invoked daily. The same is true in our daily lives. There is always a huge gap between understanding and doing.

I want to encourage you to read this book over several times. Underline the things that are the most important to you and reread those sections. My hope is that, after each reading, you will make new associations, and different parts of the book will become more important to you as you focus on your life, goals and issues. Take the time to make a difference in yourself.

So many of us live in a state of fear and despair. We aren't happy or even content with our lives. Take the time to better understand yourself. We all have it within ourselves to create the life we dream about – the life we were born to live. We can all fulfill our ultimate potential. By understanding, learning and then applying the time-tested principles within this book, you can bring about the results you seek.

When we choose to take control of ourselves, our actions, thoughts and desires, we become self-aware. There are basically two contributions we can make to create our place in society. The first is to work to our maximum ability and use what we have inside of us. The second is to help those around us to do the same. If we could all live up to that standard, the world would indeed be a better place. This book was created as a working tool for those interested in moving their lives forward. If this book helps you to do that, then we both will have succeeded.

You can learn anything you need to learn and achieve any goal you want by finding out what others before you have done to get the results they wanted.

What You Can Learn From This Book

If You Want A Better Life. Consider what is holding you back. Discover what is keeping you from getting everything you need/want. Get rid of the anchors that stop your ship from sailing. Rid yourself of fear and negativity, and take positive steps to become more achievement-oriented and optimistic. Believe in yourself and take courage in your convictions. Dream big and follow your dreams to create the fulfilling life you deserve.

If You Are A Student. This book contains information that is vital to your success, no matter which direction in life you choose. You can never be overly prepared to dream, plan, and take action! This is the time in your life to develop a keen focus about what you want and who can help you get there. Learn to expect the best but be prepared for the worst. The time management section of this book is extremely important for those adjusting to being on their own schedules without someone else controlling the pace.

If You Are A Manager Or Teacher. You are a powerful and key player/contributor in the shaping of people's lives. Your manner of communication, matching skills and gestures have an impact on those you teach or those who report to you. Your personal growth, expectations and ability to change are directly related to their success.

If You Are In Sales. Expect the best from others even though you may not always get it. Research suggests that the best salespeople are the most optimistic. They do not take rejection personally but accept it as part of the job and use it to improve their next sale. Salespeople need to have strong time management and goal-setting skills, habits that lead to success.

If You Are An Executive. Being at the top, it's important to understand the communication styles of those who report to you, to exhibit strong leadership skills, and to know when and how to take action. Executives and leaders must have both short- and long-term visions and stick to them. Executives also need to develop a values-based sense of teamwork through others.

Everyone. This book contains some formulas and explanations to help you assess where you currently are in life and *plan* how to get to where you want to be. This book is not about making any type of judgment. If you are not where you want to be, it's all right. What is not all right is staying there! Learn to take action for your own good, not because you feel like you should or to please others. Please yourself and become who you are capable of being.

I'm Getting Ready

No one can give you a sense of purpose.

Many of us are not content with our circumstances. Maybe it's our relationships, financial situation, job, health or physical condition. The point is that just about every one of us has an issue in our lives that is not as we would ideally like it to be. That's ok — that's life! The tough part comes when we let our issues/problems overwhelm us and we stop trying to find solutions.

As is true for many of you reading this book, my life did not start out a bed of roses. I grew up in the Pennsylvania-New Jersey area. My parents separated when I was two years old. There were years of moving around, including living overseas and a lengthy custody battle where, in the end, I went to live with my father. From the time I can remember, my father moved from one low-paying job to another. Money was always an issue, and we did without a lot of material possessions. I started working when I was fourteen to make extra money for myself. I started a car washing business and, over the years, was a lifeguard, lawn maintenance worker and deli worker. I went to college on a partial scholarship and worked full-time to support myself. No one handed me anything on a silver platter. In order to earn a Master's degree, I became a graduate assistant. I earned $699.00 a month, and my rent was half of that. I still remember going to the grocery store the last week of the month with about $10.00 for food for the week. One summer, to save money, I lived in my office at the university. In some ways, it wasn't too bad. I had a refrigerator, a two-burner hot plate, a sofa and a shower. In 1992, my 1978 Chevy Nova served as my transportation as well as my locker (clean clothes on the back seat, dirty clothes in the trunk). In other words, I am painfully aware of what it's like to scrape by.

After earning my Master's degree, I got a job teaching in a public school system. I moved up in the world by getting an apartment with two of my friends. During the day, I taught public school, rushed home to shower and eat before heading to the University of Houston's full-time Doctoral program at night. Upon receiving my Doctorate degree, I changed from teaching in the public school system to collegiate education and taught in two state school systems (New Hampshire and Pennsylvania). Over the years, I have come to realize my passion for education. I have read hundreds of books, attended countless seminars, and listened to thousands of hours of audiotapes in an effort to uncover the principles of success. I've sifted through specific material, extracted what I believe made the most sense, and subsequently applied those principles to my own life. This book is a culmination of what I found to be most useful in my own life, as well as what I've learned from the examples of others.

I believe that we can all find our success. Others, facing far greater challenges than you or I, have found their success and, with it, a life of fulfillment. It is not an easy path, but the journey is possible. I encourage you to take this journey; the rewards will be worth it!

We Are All On a Journey That We're Not Prepared For

To begin with, to take this journey, we must be honest with ourselves about what we want in life. We must determine what success means to us. As a guide, consider the following questions:

- Who do you know who is successful?
- Why do you think they are successful?
- What have they done to become successful?
- Do you emulate these people?
- What are you willing to do to achieve this level of success?
- What are you not willing to do?

How can we be assured that we will be successful? Because "the system" works. The principles consistently work if you follow them, just as an individual who buys a franchise with a solid track record and follows the blueprint that's been laid out can make money.

There are no real limits on what we can accomplish with the exception of those limits we create in our own minds. If you choose to become successful, however you define it, nothing can stop you. You can learn what you need to learn. Very often you can find mentors to show you the way.

Will it be easy? No, but would you really expect it to be? Everything that is worthwhile in life takes effort and a degree of sacrifice. Anything is possible if you want it badly enough and put in enough time and energy. Once you find your success, you will find that it was indeed worth the sacrifice.

Thinking Guides Us

From this point on, refuse to make excuses or justify behaviors that have prevented you from moving forward. Every time you blame others or make excuses, you give your power to someone else. Think about and see yourself "steering your own ship." You are, after all, completely in charge of your own life – now take charge!

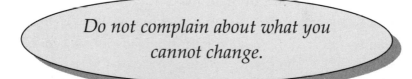

Do not complain about what you cannot change.

If what is holding you back is in the past, let it go, move forward, and focus on the present and the future. Learn how to create meaningful and realistic goals for yourself. The very act of thinking optimistically is not only constructive but also progress in the right direction.

The quality of our thinking determines the quality of our lives. We cannot truly appreciate success if we have not failed, as we would also not fully appreciate our health if we were never sick. However, keep in mind that the same walls that prevent disappointment also keep out happiness. Have you ever heard the phrase, "Better to have loved and lost than not to have loved?" Recognize that not everything we try will work out. But that shouldn't be an excuse for not trying. Make an effort to welcome new experiences that life offers. You never know when the experience that will make the difference might come along.

> Like the toy soldier said, "I wish someone would come by and wind me up." But what if they don't show up? You've got to have a better plan.

We can't wait for someone else to change our situation. It's ultimately what we do that makes the differences. The best motivation is self-motivation. Sitting on the sidelines waiting for everything to align perfectly leads to . . . a lot of waiting.

If we wait for the perfect opportunity, it may never come. It's time to stop waiting for:

- Permission from our parents, siblings, spouses and coworkers
- More self-confidence

- The "right" time
- Someone else to change
- The kids to grow up
- A new supervisor or management team at work
- The weather to change
- The "right" political climate
- Interest rates to go up/down
- All of your questions to be answered
- Fear of failure to diminish

Since the perfect situation seldom appears, the best you can do to move toward success is to make an informed decision with the information you have and go forward. One of the best metaphors I know about self-motivation is from a story I heard long ago:

> *Years ago, there was a flood. Everyone in the area gathered what they could and left for higher ground. As the waters started to rise, the police knocked at one man's door.*
>
> *The policeman said, "The waters are rising. It's time to go."*
>
> *The young man replied that he would be okay and that he wasn't leaving because God would take care of him.*
>
> *The rains continued, and the waters rose.*
>
> *The young man moved to the second floor of his home to avoid the rising water. A boat passing by stopped when neighbors on board saw the candles lit in the window.*
>
> *One neighbor said to the young man, "The waters are rising. It's time to go."*

The young man replied that we would be okay and that he wasn't leaving because God would take care of him.

As the hours passed, the young man was forced to move outside to the roof as the flood waters kept rising.

After he had been waiting on the roof for a couple of hours, the National Guard went by in a boat. The guardsman said, "The waters are rising. It's time to go. We won't have time to come back again."

The young man replied that he would be okay and that he wasn't leaving because God would take care of him.

As the boat departed without him, he was sure everything would be okay.

Days later, as the flood waters subsided, the young man's lifeless body was found.

When the man got to heaven, he was confused. How did this happen?   As he approached Heaven's gates, he asked St. Peter, "What happened? I was supposed to be taken care of."

St. Peter replied, "How many different ways were we supposed to send help? We tried four different times, including two boats. How did you not get the message?"

Many times, we wait for what we perceive to be the "right" opportunity when, in actuality, we are surrounded by opportunity, or the opportunity presents itself and we lack the strength or courage to take action.

What Are We Getting?

At a basic level, all actions are associated with either receiving pleasure or avoiding pain.   While examining ourselves through our own introspective questioning, consider these two opposing forces. If we want to change, we should consider several questions. What do our current actions provide us with? Are our current actions affording us pleasure? If so, why change? If we desire change, we must recast our old actions as undesirable and work to associate new actions with pleasure. If our actions result in enough pain, we will elect to change. Think about it. You frequently hear about people who have engaged in certain destructive behaviors for years, and one day a new stimulus causes them to completely abandon their old patterns of behavior without looking back.

I have a friend whom I have known for more than twenty years.   Throughout our relationship, he and his family members have always been significantly overweight.   In short, eating and drinking to excess was providing him satisfaction (pleasure) to some degree. While his weight bothered him over the years, it didn't bother him enough to make any substantial, lasting changes. This past year, he went to see his physician for an annual physical and was informed that he weighed 350 lbs. He later shared with me that, when he heard this, something inside of him "just snapped."   What was previously a source of pleasure suddenly was the cause of immense pain. It was at that moment that he decided he was just too heavy and did not want to continue down this path. He began an exercise program and has remained dedicated to working out at the gym four or five days a week for over a year now. He also educated himself about healthy eating and has drastically modified his eating habits. I am happy to report that, seventeen months after starting his exercise and weight loss program, he has lost over 135 pounds. In fact, he even ran a 5K and has another scheduled in the near future.

What happened to this person? He had been heavy for the majority of his life. Why did weighing that particular weight catapult him into action? I would speculate that he had been getting some degree of satisfaction from eating and drinking, even though he would have preferred weighing less, yet, at the point of weighing 350 lbs., there was a mental shift. What once provided pleasure suddenly became the source of intense pain. To avoid the pain, he took drastic action.

Law of the Farm

Hall of Fame basketball legend John Wooden, in his book *They Call me Coach*, talks about the "law of the farm." Farming is a process, and the work to be done is determined by the time of year. The soil must be prepared and fertilized. Then it must be cultivated. Quality seed is planted. Once the seeding is done, it's time to water the seeds and pull out the weeds. Finally, it is time to harvest. The harvest is the payoff for all the hard work on the front end.

The law of the farm dictates that there are no shortcuts!

Every step along the way is important, and each must be done in the correct order. Even if you do each step properly, completing them in the wrong order will result in a poor crop. Many times, we question ourselves because we think we are doing everything right and yet still do not make the desired progress. Sometimes, it is simply a matter of making a few minor changes, and we can be on our way to the results we desire.

If the farmer procrastinates and doesn't plant at the right time of the year, no amount of desire or need will change the outcome. The harvest will still be a failure.

We can get away with procrastinating and cramming some of the time, but, in the end, there will be negative consequences, just like those endured by the farmer who plants late or doesn't weed. The expression, "We reap what we sow," goes back to the Bible; it is hardly a new concept or a difficult one to understand. Yet we still procrastinate and cram and wonder why we didn't achieve the desired results.

Life continuously follows the cycle of the seasons. We can't change the seasons, but we can change ourselves. Just saying "I sure hope things will change" isn't going to make it happen. Hoping for change puts the onus on situations or people we don't control. We have to make it happen for ourselves. I know that isn't always favorable and means that we have to work hard, but it can also be positive if we realize that, no matter how bad things are, we can do a lot to create positive changes for ourselves.

Make the Best of the Seasons

Just as there is a cycle of seasons, there is an ebb and flow to our lives. When things are at a low ebb, hoping it isn't the case won't make it change. Without planning, we are unprepared.

Sometimes we have to accept that situations may be out of our control. That does not mean, however, that we should not plan.

When we have a plan, we are ready to face both the positive and negative surges life has in store.

We need to learn how to cope with the season of winter in our lives. Know that down time and discouragement will come; it's okay, and it happens to everyone. It's how we deal with it that is important. Nights are long in the winter. We can't just discard the calendar. That won't change the facts. These are the times to work on ourselves, to become stronger and wiser and to be prepared for opportunity when it arises.

Spring always follows winter. Take advantage of the spring and the longer days. Spring is the season of opportunity. Plant in the spring. Seize the day. Be ready when your time comes. Nothing is worse than not being ready to take advantage of an opportunity when it presents itself.

Summer is the time to nourish and protect. The summer sun can bring life, but it can also be threatening. For every opportunity presented, a possible threat also exists. We must have the correct combination of sun and water. The sun can bring excitement and energy. Water provides rest and replenishment. One without the other can lead to disaster. Be aware. Being complacent can also potentially cause harm. The sun can burn the crop without proper watering; insects and weeds can also ruin your garden.

In the fall, we reap our reward and enjoy the crops. It's time to examine the results. It's time to take responsibility. Figuratively speaking, if our garden did not turn out the way we had hoped, it's not because of the sunshine or rain or soil. It is not the fault of the seasons; ultimately, what is produced is a result of our action or inaction. And if it turns out well, enjoy it.

- ◆ **Winter:** Identify two of your failures and frustrations. How did you deal with them?
- ◆ **Spring:** How do you prepare for potential opportunities when they present themselves?
- ◆ **Summer:** How are you protecting and nourishing your opportunities?
- ◆ **Fall:** Examine the fruits of your labor. What have your efforts produced? What do you see?

Doing Things in Season: Rooting Out Procrastination

What we choose to do is an indicator of what we value, find ourselves capable of doing, or need/prefer doing. We have all said at times, "I'm not procrastinating. I'm just too busy." While we might indeed be busy, it is important to look at the tasks that we complete and those we choose to avoid. How can we deal with our feelings that a task is too much for us? To start, break it down into small steps. If we can create "small wins" for ourselves, we create a feeling of possibility. From there, we can develop momentum and work toward what we need/wish to accomplish.

Have you ever noticed how someone can procrastinate for a period of time and then all of a sudden take action?

Many times, we procrastinate because the task is unpleasant. We just don't want to do it. What's the best way to deal with this situation? Consider the pain/pleasure principle. What will happen if we choose not to address the unpleasant task? We must either make accomplishing the task pleasurable or make not accomplishing the task even more uncomfortable than completing it. If we can find answers to these questions, we can move ourselves forward more quickly. For instance, many of us put off filing our income taxes. The pain of dealing with the situation is enough to cause us to avoid it. Who wants to give more of our hard-earned money to the government? But something happens around the beginning of April. The pain of not doing our taxes starts to build. As April 15 approaches, the pain shifts, and suddenly the prospect of not finishing our tax forms becomes more painful than filling them out.

What decisions are you feeling reluctant to make? Procrastination affects us all to some degree. You are probably aware that, at times, you are inclined to put off a task. Regardless of what the reasons are for procrastinating, there are really only a couple of solutions. Identify *what* you have been putting off and *how* you can address it. The key to handling procrastination is to take action. Setting a deadline (when) is the best way to get started. Once we set a deadline, we set a plan in motion. The more quickly we take action, the sooner we are on our way to our destination. Notice that I did not say that the plan we selected would work. Often, we make mistakes on the way to our destination. How many times have you gotten lost driving somewhere? In most cases, even getting lost brings us closer to our destination than just sitting in our driveway hoping the destination will come to us or hoping we'll have all we think we need before we set out.

There are only two reasons for not getting something we decide we want. **The first reason is that we do not want it badly enough.** I know this statement may not ring true at first. Everyone who wants something must want it badly enough, right? Let's examine the following example. You may say that you have always wanted to be a millionaire. If you were a millionaire, your financial picture would be clear, and you would be financially secure. I can understand your desire, but I would ask: What action/s have you taken to make it a reality? If you are not financially secure, why not? Do you associate with those who are wealthy? How would doing so affect your opportunities or increase your knowledge base related to money? Do you work with financial advisors and/or planners? Do you read about how to save and invest wisely? Do you do what financially secure people do? Books like the *Millionaire Next Door* spell out, in detail, how millionaires live, how they spend, and how they buy. If you have said "no" to these questions, it is no wonder you are not a millionaire. What is worse, unless someone leaves you a sizeable amount of money, chances are you will not become a millionaire because perhaps you do not want it badly enough. If you did, you would find time to increase your opportunities, research your options, and work on changing your spending habits. The good news is that, at any point, we can decide to change and try a different path. According to Jim Rohn, a business philosopher, "Unless you change how you are, you will always have what you've got." Different actions produce different results, and we can take action any time we choose.

The second reason for not getting something we want it is that we can't get ourselves to take consistent action. I know many people who have great dreams and have thought out and even planned for what they want. The missing link is a lack of consistent effort. Remember it's an apple a day, not five apples on Monday and none until Saturday. The effort and results of each day are important.

Below is an exercise to address procrastination. It may help identify a smaller project or task that you've been putting off. Then apply this exercise to a larger, long-term project or task you've been meaning to tackle.

Ways to Handle Procrastination

1. Focus on a project or task you have procrastinated doing for more than one year.
2. List the feelings that you associate with doing this project or task.

Ways to Handle Procrastination (cont.)

3. List the feelings you associate with **not** doing this project or task.

4. List the physical and economic factors involved in completing this project or task (cost).

5. List the physical and economic costs of **not** doing this project or task.

6. What will change if you complete this project or task?

7. Which of these changes are positive? Which are negative?

8. What are the first three things you need to do to get closer to completing this project or task?

9. What is a realistic deadline for completing this project or task?

10. List at least three rewards that will come from completing this project or task.

As you may have noticed while working on the above checklist, we often follow a pattern when it comes to procrastination. We may put off only certain tasks or many. It could be that fear causes our inaction. It's also easy to put off tasks by telling ourselves that they aren't likely to "meet our high standards." Perhaps we have too much "on our plate," so inevitably, we postpone some tasks. We may procrastinate completing a project until time is short, believing that we work better under pressure, using pressure as a motivating force. Living life at this speed can eventually catch up with us (leading to stress, health problems, financial issues, lack of promotion, etc.).

To address our own patterns of procrastination, it often helps to brainstorm. For instance, ask yourself, "What is it about this task that causes me to procrastinate?" Then consider ways to overcome it. Remember, procrastination is a symptom, not a cause. If you procrastinate, don't give yourself a hard time about it; just make the decision to act. If you can get to the root cause, it will be easier to understand and take action. Think of a task you have completed without procrastinating. What made this task easy to complete?

I Just Don't Want To?

Johnny's father walked into his son's room at six in the morning and said, "Johnny, get up. It's time for school!"

Johnny did not stir.

His father yelled again, "It's time for school!"

Once again no response.

Eventually, Johnny's father shook him, saying, "Johnny, it's time to get up and get ready for school."

This time, Johnny emphatically stated, "I'm not going. There are two thousand kids at that school and every one of them hates me. All the teachers hate me too. I saw a bunch of them talking and looking at me. I know they all hate me, so I'm not going to school."

Again Johnny's father yelled, "Get to school!"

"But, dad, why are you so mean to me?"

"Johnny, for two reasons," his dad responded. "First, you are fifty three years old. Second, you're the principal."

Most of us have days like Johnny's when we don't want to go to school or work or follow through on a commitment we have made. There are times when we just want to escape from what we need or are expected to do. These are the times to keep in mind that taking some action — however small — is making progress.

If a task is overwhelming or unpleasant, we may tend to procrastinate. We don't procrastinate by accident. There are reasons why we act, as well as reasons why we do not. If we put something off or "forget" to do it, it's simply because it wasn't important enough to us at the time or we make the task more of a chore than it needs to be and approach it with a negative state of mind. But often, when we create a deadline for ourselves, we are more likely to take action. We get away from "someday" and "when I get to it." Creating a deadline makes dealing with the task more real. Yet setting a deadline doesn't mean that it cannot be changed or modified. What it does is create a timeframe instead of a nebulous "someday."

Start with the task that you have been putting off and break it into small, manageable steps. Write out the steps you need to take to complete the task. As you finish each step, you will already be aware of the next step, making it more difficult to procrastinate. Get started and remember to allow yourself to enjoy the feeling of success upon completion of each step in the process. Carry this feeling of success forward, build on it, and allow it to serve as a source of inspiration/motivation.

For example, if your goal is to save money for a down payment on a house, the key is to determine approximately how much money you will need. Then, determine how much you can afford to set aside on a regular basis. Next, figure out how many months you will need to stay on this course to have the amount you will need. Finally, stay focused and stick to your plan. A good plan followed consistently over time will produce the desired results.

> *What we need to remember is that, no matter where we are today, we can be in a better place tomorrow and in the future.*

Eventually, we reach a point when we decide we have a problem. This may come in the form of a foreclosure notice, being served with divorce papers, or maybe just a realization that things are not the way we want them to be, such as finding oneself in a job with little hope of advancement. This disparity, between where we want to be and where we actually are, typically does not happen in a day, a week or even a month. It is often the cumulative effect of poor decision-making or inaction over time.

Maybe we have been spending money we do not have, not paying enough attention to a significant other, or coasting along and not putting in the effort to make personal improvements. While we cannot always control all aspects of a given situation, we can all make self-improvements and change the way we feel about ourselves if we follow a winning formula.

Keep It Simple: It's All in the Fundamentals

Following the fundamentals is the key to success, in business and in life. If you are a quick learner and like everything condensed to the Cliff's Notes version, you will be happy to know that the fundamentals don't change — and they are easy to understand. If we master the basics in any field – be it the specialized field of business or overall "field of life" — we can succeed. How could we not?

Make things as simple as possible. Simple is easy to understand. The more complex something is, the more chance of error. Remember the seasons. There is a time and place for everything. Realizing that we can all get "bogged down" from time to time is also easy to understand. Likewise, the importance of forcing ourselves to take action by taking small steps is easily understood and simple to employ.

> *The more we can simplify our lives, the more success we can achieve.*

Questions for Self-Assessment

1. When in your life have you created a plan for yourself?

2. Did you follow it? If not, what happened?

3. What changes did you need to make over time?

4. What were your results?

5. Why did you get the results that you did?

6. What are you procrastinating about that you know needs attention? Pick one area or topic.

7. What is it about the task that you find overwhelming, unpleasant, or both?

8. What strategies can you implement to help you in getting "unstuck" and moving forward?

9. What small steps can you take right now to begin moving forward?

2

Who Are We, Really?

> *Be more concerned with your character than your reputation,*
> *because your character is what you really are, while your*
> *reputation is merely what others think you are.*
> *- John Wooden*

Ideally, our actions and values should be congruent one hundred percent of the time. In reality, however, that is often not the case. When we make choices incongruent with our value system or sense of self, it creates inner conflict. We may feel unsettled because our actions do not reflect our feelings or vice versa. This will continue unless we modify our behavior (e.g., actions/goals) so that they are "in line" or consistent with our values.

Many people are unclear about their goals and values. Yet the mark of successful people is that they know who they are, what they believe in, what they stand for — and their actions reflect their values. It is because of this that so many successful individuals have gone further and accomplished more, even with potentially fewer opportunities and, in some cases, less innate ability and aptitude.

Who Am I?

The only real approval that matters is that which comes from inside ourselves. If we feel unworthy of success, most likely we will achieve less than what we deserve. Whom would you rather spend time with: someone who is pessimistic and suspicious, always assuming the worst is going to happen, or someone who is optimistic and confident, able to face obstacles and turn them into opportunities? It's in our best interest to be as optimistic and self confident as we can.

Our own fears, perceived limitations, and self-criticism alienate us from our potential success and undermine our confidence. Self-doubt is one of the greatest obstacles to success. Too often, we defer to the opinions of others, whether consciously or unconsciously, instead of trusting ourselves or our own self image.

Perhaps we value others' opinions too highly and our own too little?

We need to make a shift from thoughts of self-doubt to those of self-belief. It is possible to be all that we want to be when we believe in ourselves and our talents and abilities.

Self-esteem is defined as "how much we like ourselves." Our self-esteem, in turn, is determined by our self-image, or the way we see and think about ourselves in our day-to-day living. Psychologists believe that, the more our situational behavior is consistent with what we believe our ideal behavior should be, the more content and at peace we will be. Conversely, whenever we act in a way that is inconsistent with our ideal behavior, we experience a negative self-image.

If we want to be more successful, we need to improve/strengthen our self-concept. We need to increase what we think we are capable of. Our self-efficacy is determined by how well we perform at what we do. The better we perform, the more confidence we will have and vice versa. Often, when we make efforts to change and stretch out of our comfort zone, we positively enhance our self-concept. Our strengthened sense of self-efficacy will also enable us to cope with failure more effectively, as we recognize a difference between the events in our life and who we are. The more we face adversity and uncertainty, the more we challenge our self-concept and grow as a result. As we learn to think, feel and act in ways that reflect our values and ideal sense of self, our efficacy and confidence increases and vice-versa.

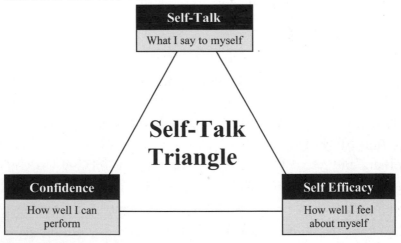

Control Begins with Ourselves

To take the kind of consistent action that fosters confidence and a positive self-concept, we need to cultivate self-control.   Our minds work in the direction of our dominant thoughts. Self-control is our inner discipline that helps guide us when we want to veer off-course.   Self-control reminds us not to eat that extra donut. It reminds us to exercise daily.   Self-control reminds us not to spend money unwisely.   Our self-control keeps us faithful to our partner when temptation arises.

The stronger our self-control, the more likely we are to succeed. In fact, it is virtually impossible to succeed without self-control.

"Everything I have accomplished has come about because of my self-control," bestselling author Denis Waitley has said.

No one has a problem when everything is going smoothly. But, as Hubert Humphrey said, "A smooth sea never made a skillful mariner." Anyone can steer the ship in calm waters.   Maintaining self-control during the tough times is the key. What do you do when things heat up? Do you become defensive and attack others? Do you blame others and avoid personally taking responsibility? Do you focus on the negative aspects rather than the positive? The more intense the pressure, the more self-control is necessary. We are, by nature, emotional creatures.   Exhibiting self-control allows us to more rationally approach turbulent, challenging periods.

If we are at odds with ourselves and struggle with feelings of guilt, why are we? Are our behaviors at odds with our vision and values? Are we moving toward or away from our dreams and goals? At critical moments, ask yourself if the action you are contemplating will move you toward or away from what you want. Our self-control is there to assist, not to work against us. Draw lessons from your life experiences. What went well? What needs refining? Develop a strong self-control and use it to your benefit. Take directed action and move forward the way you envision you should. The bottom line is that, when you know you've developed self-control, you are more likely to respect yourself, and, once you respect yourself, you're moving forward in the right direction.

No one can take away our self-respect. One of our deepest subconscious needs is to be accepted by others. That being the case, we need to be aware of this phenomenon but be able to get beyond it.

> *"The real key to success is within us. No one can give it to us or take it away. We hold our destiny in our hands,"*
> - Ronald Reagan.

Since self-respect comes from within, what we think about ourselves is what really matters. If, as John Wooden says, "Success is peace of mind that is a direct result of self

34 Christopher Saffici

satisfaction in knowing you gave your best effort to become the best of which you are capable," without self-control, peace of mind is unattainable. If we do our best, we have no regrets. We have given our all and — win or lose — we can rest assured that we have acted in accordance with our values and dreams.

Low Self-Esteem

There are three major causes of low self-esteem. The first is a series of self-defeating concepts, beliefs and values that we have accepted from our parents and family members. The second is a series of putdowns, received through our pre-adolescent and adolescent years from authority figures and from those whose opinions we value, such as friends and peers. The third stems from negative conditioning with an overemphasis on guilt and unworthiness. While there are many other contributing factors to low self-esteem, these three seem to be most common.

> *The strongest single contributing factor to children's self-esteem is the self-esteem of their parental figures.*

When influential adults labor under false concepts, values and beliefs, these are passed on to children through attitudes and behaviors. Specifically, if our parents feel inadequate, we are likely to develop a negative self-image and suffer from feelings of worthlessness as children and, ultimately, as adults as well. As a result, we may have tremendous difficulty coping with even the simplest problems at home, at work, in school and in our relationships with others.

Frequently, it begins as we make mistakes as children and are told that we are "bad." The truth is: there is no such thing as a "bad child." As part of the learning process, children make mistakes and poor choices. Obviously, there are certain things that a child should not do, for which reasonable disciplinary action is necessary. But these, in and of themselves, do not make a child "good" or "bad." If children are not helped to understand the difference between being a bad person and making poor choices, they develop feelings of inferiority which become programmed into their minds subconsciously. These feelings will manifest themselves as shame, self-condemnation, remorse, guilt and feelings of inadequacy, which result in negative feelings of self-worth and low self-esteem.

Low or poor self-esteem can be further indoctrinated through the common habit of belittling by comparison. It could be parents comparing a child to a sibling or someone outside the family, resulting in the child's own sense of inferiority being intensified. In light of the flaws he has come to accept as part of his own make-up, he compares himself to children of the same age whom he admires and, sadly, comes up short.

Parents often fail to appreciate and validate their children's uniqueness. All too many parents pay little regard to their children's feelings, desires or opinions, and the Victorian notion that "children should be seen and not heard" is still alive and well in many families. Insecure parents, for example, may take a child's assertion of uniqueness or autonomy as a personal affront or a sign of out-and-out disrespect.

It is also a disturbing phenomenon when parents unconsciously live their lives vicariously through their children. This also can have an extremely negative impact on children. Having decided that their children should be everything the parents secretly yearned to be and are not, they push the children to fulfill parental unmet goals, needs or desires. This is especially prevalent in education and sport settings. Of course, this happens at the child's expense. Parents may fail to recognize that the child is not only unable or unwilling to meet their expectations but also that he should not be expected to do so. What children learn in these situations is that it is not enough to be who they are; they are not "good enough" the way they are. This is a seriously damaging major blow to a healthy self-esteem.

Playing Out Low Self-Esteem

Blaming and Complaining – When our self-esteem is fragile, we blame and complain to others as we refuse to accept the fact that we each are responsible for what happens in our lives. It is much easier to blame someone else than to say, "I am the problem; I must change." People who constantly complain and blame others clearly feel inadequate and need to build themselves up by putting others down.

Fault Finding – We find fault with others because they do not accept or comply with our set of values. We then compensate for feelings of inadequacy by trying to make ourselves right and them wrong. We may have learned from others that someone must be blamed.

Need for Attention and Approval – When our self-esteem is low, we have an overwhelming and endless need for attention and approval. If we are unable to recognize and appreciate ourselves as worthy, adequate individuals, we constantly seek affirmation/validation from others and demand that they accept and approve of us.

Lack of Close Friends – People with low self-esteem often do not have close friends. Because they do not like themselves, they generally choose to be either "loners," living their lives apart from others, or manifest the opposite behavior pattern and become aggressive and overpowering or invest only superficially in relationships.   This leaves them feeling lonely and unfulfilled. Neither personality is conducive to meaningful friendship.

Need to Win – If we have an exaggerated need to win or to be right all the time, we may suffer from a need to prove ourselves to those around us. We may try to do this through our achievements. Our motivation becomes to receive the acceptance and approval of others or maybe just to convince ourselves that we are "okay."   The idea of being "better than" the next person is not the same as striving to do our best.

Overindulgence – People who do not like themselves may try to satisfy their needs by overeating or drinking or by overindulging through other means. Feeling deprived and hurt, they seek mental and physical stimuli to dull the pain. They overeat, take drugs, drink or smoke excessively to cover up their emotional pain and desperate need for approval. Overindulgence provides only a temporary escape from facing reality and a need to change.

Greed and Selfishness – Those who are overly selfish may have feelings of inadequacy. They become absorbed in their own needs and desires, which they are desperate to fulfill (at any cost) to compensate for their lack of self-worth. They seldom have the time, interest or capacity to care for others, even with the people whom they claim to love.

Putting up a Public Persona – Those who put up a false front often feel inferior to those around them. To conceal this, they often name drop, boast, or exhibit such nervous mannerisms as a loud voice or forced laughter. They work hard not to let anyone know the real "x" so as to hide how they truly feel about themselves. In an effort to hide their feelings of inferiority, they put up a false front to keep others from seeing them as they really are.

Fear of Criticism

One of the most common offshoots of a poor self-esteem is the fear of criticism. How we react to criticism determines whether we will move forward or "get stuck." When we are criticized, we could respond in a variety of ways. If we agree that the critiques are accurate, we can listen and consider making changes as quickly as possible. If we disagree with the criticism, we have other options. When we are criticized, it makes sense to first consider the source. Do we value this person's opinion? Do we have to listen to this person because s/he is an authority figure? Do we simply wish to ignore the comments? And why?

> *If we allow criticism to lead to worry and self-doubt, we can become so anxious about making mistakes that we become unable to make decisions or take action.*

The same is true of self-criticism. In fact, self-criticism can be even more destructive because it often takes place on a subconscious level. Keep in mind that criticism doesn't have to be direct; it can be implied or even imagined.

As president, Abraham Lincoln faced far more criticism from considerably more people than most of us ever will in a lifetime. Here's what he had to say about the experience: "If I were to try and read, much less answer, all the attacks made on me, this shop might as well be closed for another business. I do the very best I know how, the very best I can, and I mean to keep doing so until the end. If the end brings me out all right, what is said against me won't amount to anything. If the end brings me out wrong, then ten angels swearing I was right would make no difference." You don't have to run for president to take these words to heart: use criticism to grow and to improve, but do not allow it to hold you back.

Responding to Criticism

How you use criticism has a lot to do with how you take it. The following examples show the shades of difference between a self-harming response and a self-affirming response. The first example involves direct verbal criticism; the other three involve actions that could be taken as indirect criticism.

Situation	Feedback	Old Response	New Response
You lose an account	Boss yells at you	I always make mistakes	I can learn from this
Marital problems	Spouse leaves you	I'm no good	We both need to work towards change. How can I change myself?
Lost money	Financial difficulties	I shouldn't even try	I need better advice to get ahead
Overate during first pregnancy	Gained 55 lbs.	I'm not disciplined	I need to work toward what my goal weight is

When you receive what you perceive to be negative evaluation or feedback, try asking yourself the following questions as a way of forming a positive response to criticism:

- How else can I interpret the feedback?
- Is this the only interpretation I can make from this comment or reaction? What would be the optimistic view on this comment or response?
- Why do I think this way about it?
- Am I sure the feedback was intended to be negative?
- Did I really listen to or think about the feedback, or am I just reacting to it on an emotional level?

Perceiving Yourself as a Success

Individuals with strong self-esteem think long-term. While you're working on developing an inward sense of self-esteem, it's important to try on the external features of healthy self-esteem. In twelve-step programs, there's a saying, "Act as if . . ." you are successful, happy, fun to be around, etc. That's because the inside and the outside are mutually reinforcing. You can always spot people with a poor sense of self-esteem. They blame and criticize others. They inflate themselves by putting others down. They feel as though no one understands their problems or dilemmas. Those who yell or scream the most are often the most fragile themselves.

Sit down and write a description of yourself. Take time to relax and picture the "ideal you." Write down exactly how you would look and feel and what you would do with a fully positive self-image. For instance, would you:

- ◆ Smile more often?
- ◆ Maintain good posture, with head up and shoulders square?
- ◆ Assume that others like you?
- ◆ Focus only on the positive in your conversation?

Emotions can be difficult to navigate, yet their mastery is key to self-control and, ultimately, to gaining an increased sense of self-esteem. Remember to think of emotions as energy in motion. Are you moving toward who you want to be or away from it? If your emotions are preventing you from taking positive action, shift your focus. When you feel angry, use relaxation techniques such as conscious breathing. When you feel discouraged, try taking stock of your successes, which generally outnumber the failures. When overwhelmed by frustration, shift your focus to trying alternative approaches to a problem. If you feel resentful toward someone, work at forgiving that person; it can release a lot of negative energy. Most importantly, when negative emotions arise, remind yourself that you are not the emotion.

Life has a way of challenging even the healthiest self-esteem, let alone one that is "in formation." If you're having trouble maintaining a healthy self-esteem, determine what action is necessary to restore it. When you are criticized, ask yourself if it's valid. If so, take corrective action. If not, forget it and keep moving forward. Here are a few other strategies for shoring up your self-esteem when it takes a hit:

- When your buttons get pushed, delay your response.
- Recognize that we all make mistakes and that it allows for personal growth.
- When others appear to doubt you, remember that it is *their* doubt, not yours.
- When you become frustrated, relax, take a deep breath, or even walk away for a while.
- When you become discouraged, remember that it is a short-term emotion.

We all must work with what we have and develop skills and strengths we don't have. If you need to work at developing a stronger self-esteem, know that you're not alone. For all the reasons I've shared, a healthy self-esteem is, unfortunately, not something we are all equipped with as we enter the world in young adulthood. But making sure that we strengthen/enhance it ourselves is something we must do for ourselves.

What Do You Stand For?

With a stronger self-esteem, we are able to identify and act from our values. Values consist of our core qualities and beliefs. What are your values?

> Our character is realized and solidified when we live our life consistently with our values.

Almost all religious and philosophical traditions, in seeking out the ways to wisdom and knowledge, encourage the cultivation of key values including courage, love, temperance and justice. Every choice or decision we make is based on our value system. Our values are always demonstrated in our actions. Mark Twain said, "Always do right. That will gratify some of the people and astonish the rest."

Pay attention to your actions, especially when you are under pressure. It is only when we clearly understand our values and rank them that we are equipped to plan for success. A key to determining how important a value is on your personal hierarchy is by how much time, money or emotion you invest in it. If, for example, you value your time spent with your children, you probably have made changes in your schedule to make that happen.

The point I am making is that our goals must be consistent with our values and vice-versa. This is why revisiting and clarifying our values is the starting point to success and peak performance. Clarifying our values requires us to think through what we really value in life. Once we have determined what is most important to us, we have created our focal point. Everything else that we do should be based on our value system and the priority we give to certain values over others.

Many people work hard to achieve goals — such as financial security — only to find, at the end of the day, that they don't really enjoy what they are getting in return. They ask, "Is this all there is?" or "What happened?" These types of scenarios occur when their accomplishments are not consistent with their value system. When our goals are not congruent with our values, it's as if we have two horses pulling in opposite directions. Let me explain. Most people agree that goals can basically be described as what we are striving for and making plans to achieve. They are our objectives. Often, they are more easily measured than values. Values, on the other hand, are what is important or significant to us - what we value in the long-term. Ideally, we want our top five goals to be in line with our top five values. The significance may not seem apparent at first, but let me share an example with you that demonstrates this idea more clearly.

After a seminar I taught, Laura came to me and said that she loved her job but that, for some reason, achieving her career goals seemed to be a real struggle lately. In inquiring about her goals, I learned that she had recently revised her career goals. She had established very clear and defined goals. Her top three were to expand the sales territory, increase her income, and to train new sales people within the territory.

Next, I asked Laura about her values. She responded by looking at me as if I was speaking in a foreign language. I explained to her that values are those intangible things that are important to us. Being a religious and family person, Laura quickly and confidently stated that her top three values were her relationship with her husband, the well-being of her children, and her spirituality.

Then it was time to explore what she was doing to realize her career goals. She reported that she was traveling more, going out of town frequently, even on weekends, which meant missing church services and her son's baseball games. It quickly became apparent that Laura's goals were not congruent with her values. In fact, Laura's goals were taking her away from what she valued most. Recognizing this actually made the solution fairly simple. Laura rearranged her schedule and her career goals so that she was no longer away from home on weekends and thus was able to live and work in a way that was more consistent with her values.

How can you tell what you truly value? The answer is simple. Our values are demonstrated in our actions, especially actions under pressure. Whenever we are forced to choose between one action or another, we always act in our order of value priority. Some people confuse values with religion. Although religion relates to a value system, one could have no religious affiliations and still uphold a specific value system.

Change Is Good

As you can see, when our goals and values are incongruent, inner conflict results. These conflicts can create difficulties in making the best choices, not to mention exhaustion. Conversely, if our goals and values are in line with or in support of one another, we tend to feel more positive emotions. "When you give your brain mixed messages, you're going to get mixed results" says Anthony Robbins. This simplifies and clarifies things, at the very least.

What are your current values regarding your occupation or career? Do you believe in the values of integrity, hard work, cooperation and getting along with other people? People who subscribe to these values are likely to be more successful than those who do not.

What are your values with regard to family? Do you believe in the importance of unconditional love, mutual support, communication, respect, patience and forgiveness? People who support these values consistently in relationships are reported to be much happier than those who do not.

What are your values with regard to financial success? Do you believe in the importance of honesty, persistence, lifelong education and optimal performance? People who subscribe to these values have greater financial success than those who do not. They also tend to achieve financial success more quickly.

What about health? Do you believe in the importance of self-discipline and self-control regarding diet, rest, and exercise? Do you set high standards for health and fitness and then work to live up to those standards? It stands to reason that people who live healthier lives tend to be healthier and live longer.

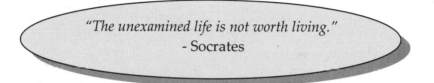

"The unexamined life is not worth living."
- Socrates

The following is a sample list of values — by no means comprehensive. Take the time to determine your top ten values. Also, rank what you value least. Identifying your values will serve as a starting point in developing a deeper understanding of yourself. This is a necessary first step in goal-setting: to begin moving in a direction that is in harmony with who you are and what you value most.

_____ Religion/Spirituality	_____ Comfort
_____ Career Advancement	_____ Independence
_____ Achievement	_____ Education
_____ Creativity	_____ Affiliations
_____ Travel	_____ Charity
_____ Longevity	_____ Meaningful job
_____ Friendships	_____ Status
_____ Health	_____ Security
_____ Family	_____ Significant Other

_____ Happiness	_____ Variety
_____ Recognition	_____ Wealth
_____ Free Time	_____ Imagination
_____ Peace	_____ Modesty
_____ Love	_____ Physical Fitness
_____ Humility	_____ Generosity
_____ Willpower	_____ Truth
_____ Respect	_____ Balance
_____Adventure	_____ Caring
_____ Courage	_____ Contribution
_____ Excellence	_____ Patience
_____ Honesty	_____ Trust

What have you learned through creating your list? Did any one value stand out for you? Did you have any values come to the surface that you have neglected over time? It is always good to stop from time to time and evaluate where we are. Are you working towards the values that you deem significant? If not, why? Take some time to think about ways to work toward the values that you feel are most important to you.

Where Do Our Values Come From?

Where do our values and beliefs come from? Our parents and family origin largely influence the development of values beginning early in childhood. From adolescence on, our friends and personal associates also influence us to some degree. Media sources such as television, advertising, the Internet have an influence as well. Some individuals have no real compass that they follow; they are obligated to no one and follow no creed. They are kings of their own castles and do as they please whenever they please. These are usually isolated, lonely individuals who maintain limited meaningful relationships. And they may even invest much energy in their own lives. Because they make few sacrifices, they do not connect and relate well with others. They are following another philosophy.

> *"I care not what others think of what I do, but I do care much about what I think of what I do."* - Theodore Roosevelt

When we consciously go against our core beliefs, inner conflict occurs. Something feels wrong or out of place. We do not feel at peace with ourselves. When this happens, our minds seek to resolve the discrepancy. Something must change. We can either reprioritize our beliefs so that they reflect our actions, or we change our actions to be consistent with our beliefs. Either way, adjustments must be made for us to be at peace with ourselves.

Last summer, my daughter and I were walking along the beach exploring. Up ahead of us several birds were flying and diving onto the beach. As we approached, the birds flew away, and we noticed a number of crab shells that had obviously been prey to these birds. One crab was stuck sideways in the sand. Evidently, it had been dropped and just happened to have landed this way. I later learned that the birds grab the crabs when the tide recedes, then they fly high into the air and drop the crabs in an attempt to crack their shells. Once that happens, they swoop down to feast. This particular crab was dropped from a high altitude but somehow landed without breaking; still, it was stuck.

I called my daughter over, and we discussed what to do. I suggested that we pick up the crab and throw him back in the ocean. My daughter didn't like that idea as she was planning on swimming in the area and was fearful of meeting the crab again. She thought we should just leave him there because, after all, the birds need dinner, too! After discussing the situation, we eventually compromised and put the crab back in the ocean, in an area where she would not be swimming.

The situation to me was my very own starfish story. In the end, it didn't really matter whether we threw the crab back or not, but it mattered deeply to that one particular crab. The differing points of view my daughter and I held about how to handle the situation reinforced for me that there was really not a clear right or wrong, but, rather, our sense of right and wrong depends on our frame of reference - or hierarchy of values.

> *We secure our friends not by accepting*
> *favors but by doing them.*
> —Thucydides

Being True to Others, Being True to Ourselves

Loyalty, whether in business or relationships, creates a feeling of connection that often supersedes even our own personal desires. Loyalty means refusing to compromise our values or beliefs for other people. Lou Holtz, former football coach at Notre Dame and the University of South Carolina, felt that the answers to the following three questions regarding loyalty and accountability have a lot to do with how successful we are in achieving our goals. Take a few minutes to reflect:

- ◆ Can people trust me to do my best?
- ◆ Am I committed to the task at hand?
- ◆ Do I care about other people and show it?

Many individuals have "situational" loyalty. They appear loyal until they are tested. They are loyal until the going gets tough. Then, they cave under the pressure of the situation. How many friendships have been destroyed due to a lack of genuine loyalty? How many marriages have failed because one or both parties were not committed to loyalty? How many problems have been created at work due to a lack of loyalty?

At the same time, we must also be loyal to ourselves and to our core beliefs, particularly at moments when loyalty to others threatens to compromise our own values. According to Henry Ward Beecher, "A man's character is the reliability of himself," and, at times, we find that we have to choose between loyalty to our values and loyalty to others. Loyalty is standing up for what we believe in, regardless of the consequences. It's imperative that we are loyal to ourselves, our deepest principles and strongest convictions.

Find Common Ground

Loyalty binds — can be defined as conflicts between loyalty to others and loyalty to our own core values. This is less likely to happen when we establish friends and associates who share our personal values. As people, we tend to like people who are like us. Find the commonalties and we will discover friends. When we become like others and hear their voices, the message, whatever it is, is better received. Become a good communicator. Be a good listener. Let others talk about themselves. We gain more insight as listeners than as talkers. When we listen effectively, by actively listening, we build rapport. When we are talking, we fill the air. We control the conversation but not the interaction. People are looking for commonality but not for those who talk without also being good listeners.

We tend to like people who "appear" to be like us. The key word is "appear." What happens when we are not like those we are talking with? What happens when we can't find commonality? What happens when we are opposites? Research suggests that opposites really don't attract, so don't count on that strategy working well for you. We must appear to be like someone else. We must use their language and their gestures. More importantly, we need to be able to understand and empathize with them even if we do not agree with them. If individuals feel heard, even if they do not get their way, they are more apt to continue dialogue and want to work toward commonality.

Successful people are not motivated to give based on what they receive in return. Their beliefs and values remain constant and motivate them regardless of payoff or popular sentiment. As we communicate our expectations to others, we influence their expectations for themselves. Individuals are more apt to listen when they observe the sacrifices and contributions made by others. People are also more prone to respond to a request for action when they are given a reason for the request. This is true for individuals of all ages. We all want to know why before we act.

> *"Evolved leaders win the trust and support of the people through their complete identification with them."*
> - Tao Te Ching

Keep an open mind toward people. Try to accept them as they are rather than demanding that they become who or what we want them to be. I have a friend whom I consider to be an eternal optimist — or a "good-finder." Whenever I inquire about someone I do not know, I can almost guarantee that his response will be the same: "He's a good guy, you'll like him." He always chooses to look for the good in people.

In business or personal relationships, believing that the other person "did the right thing" creates an unconscious desire in us to do the same. Treating others honestly and fairly will inspire them to want to do the same for us. There are exceptions to this rule, but it generally holds true. That being said, we typically treat others as they treat us. If you desire a particular result, create that result by finding the common ground with others and treating them in ways that respect their values and your own.

Our Own Personality

To bring our values and sense of self into meaningful and effective interactions with others, you'll also need to take your personality type into consideration. Undoubtedly, there are positive attributes about yourself that you find attractive, which is why you are the way you are. Looking at the chart below, what words would you use to describe your personality type? Based on the list below, are you predominantly a take-charge, friends-first, caring or competent personality?

Take-Charge	Friends-First	Caring	Competent
Initiator	Extrovert	Sensitive	Neat
Impatient	Enthusiastic	Compromiser	Prefers structure
Self-sufficient	Needs attention	Problem-solver	Reserved
Seeks responsibility	Articulate	Consistent	Looks for support from others

Obviously, these are not the only classifications for personality styles but, rather, serve as an example. Think about the strengths of your personality style. What best describes you most of the time? What are the weaknesses of your personality type?

In addition, think about how your personality style meshes with other people. What type of personality do you work best with? What personality types do you tend to clash with? The answers to these questions can help you to increase your awareness of the personality types you'll seek out to help you to reach your goals. It may also provide insight about what piece of the overall picture is missing in your personal and work life. You can then choose to work with someone who has the personality and skills in areas that are not your strength.

Keep in mind that our weaknesses are often an extension of our strengths. If we become more aware of who we are, we can seek out people whose strengths complement both our strengths and our weaknesses. We all respond positively to compliments, as well as to encouragement. We all need to feel a sense of purpose. Find out what drives others and then help them achieve it. Notice that I didn't say *find out what drives others and then give it to them.* Help them find their way, and they will be stronger for the experience.

Understanding Personality Differences

Style	Needs	Strength	Weakness
Take-Charge	Problem-solver Decision-maker Goal-oriented Communicator	Finds fault Lakes caution Dominates people Time-consuming	Control Authority Prestige Recognition
Friends-First	Team player "Good-finder" Loyal	"Iffy" follow through Lacks objectivity Possessive	Acceptance Conversation Positive reinforcement
Caring	Good listener Patient Analyzer	Avoids risks Avoids conflict Can be rigid	Security Time Precision
Competent	Accurate High standards	Procrastinates Can be critical	Time Facts

It Pays to Get Personal

Successful people recognize that life is a series of interpersonal relationships. They deal on one-on-one terms with anyone, at any level, under any circumstances, as it enables them to form bonds readily, make a positive impact, and conduct themselves successfully. When you make the effort to build relationships and find common abilities:

Others react more favorably to you. Because they haven't expected you to point out something you have in common with them or reveal a bit of personal information, they are pleasantly surprised. More importantly, they immediately feel closer to you and more receptive to whatever you have to say. Think about it: Don't you feel the same way when someone makes a personal connection with you?

People readily open up to you. Your openness gives them the confidence and courage to reveal themselves, too. As you continue to communicate on a personal level, you invariably discover more common interest on which to build a positive working relationship.

You build trust. People follow and support individuals they trust, and they are more likely to trust someone who appears genuine, approachable, and willing to reveal his or her own imperfections. People grow to trust you because you let them see who you really are and demonstrate to them that you are interested in them as people.

How to Get Personal

Work on insuring your positive attitude. Become more willing to deal with others on a personal level and search for common ground. Remember that the personal — feelings, fears, likes, dislikes, and so on — is universal. There are typically areas of common interest which help us connect with others.

Reveal enough of yourself to show your human side. I'm not referring to "spilling your guts" or sharing your deepest, darkest secrets. Perhaps relate a humorous story, confessing an error you made in your life, or share something your wife, son or mother said to demonstrate your humanness. Ask questions.   Be a good listener; afford others an opportunity to talk about themselves as well.

Respect others' privacy by maintaining confidentiality. Keep what you hear to yourself and avoid bringing it up at a later date to gain some sort of advantage. Getting personal is not a technique for manipulating others. It is a way to build trust, rapport, and effective relationships. The more successful interactions you develop with others, the more common bonds you establish. Walt Disney World describes their customer service as consistently exceeding customers' expectations. If you were to consistently exceed others expectations for you, what would happen to your interactions?

It all begins with a strong sense of self, a clear sense of what is important to you, and interested engagement with others. Getting personal and knowing who you are makes the path to your goals that much more rewarding because they help you to find and keep good company along the way.

Questions for Self-Assessment

1. What values are most important to you? Make a list of three to five of your most important values in life today. What do you really stand for?

2. Which one person has most significantly influenced your value system?

3. How would you describe that person?

4. What are your personality strengths? What qualities are you best known for among those who know you best?

5. Describe an ideal person, the person you would be if you had no limitations.

6. What one change can you make in your behavior today that would help you live in greater harmony with your values?

We Are What We Repeatedly Do

It is easier to go down a hill than up, but the view is from the top.
- Arnold Bennett

Would you agree that where you are right now is the result of your action or inaction? Are you willing to make what may seem like a difficult decision now that could improve your future? A true decision means that action flows from it. In many instances, it's not that we don't know how. It may be that, until now, you haven't been able to get yourself to take consistent action in a positive direction. Many individuals have great plans, yet never take action! Thinking is the easy part; action is where the real work is. People at rest tend to stay at rest. Conversely, on a positive note, people in motion tend to stay in motion. By making a plan and taking action, you can achieve greater success in shorter periods of time.

You Can Do It

It is essential that you believe change is possible and that goal-setting is an important part of the process. We all set the height of our own bar. We acknowledge that change is possible and that change comes from action. Next, we acknowledge that we are capable of taking action. Rarely can we succeed if we don't believe in ourselves.

Don't worry if you do not have all the details worked out before you start.

Planning is essential, but we must be able to make adjustments as situations change. If we wait until we have worked out every detail, we might never start along the journey. Remember that the greatest challenge is not in deciding to act but in taking action. The first step is the most difficult. Mile three on the treadmill is not the hardest. The hardest part is getting on in the first place. "As soon as possible" may turn out to be too late. The following questions may help you to sharpen your focus and assist in getting started.

- ♦ What is your identified area for improvement?

- ♦ What are you doing that you don't want to do or failing to do that you would like to do?

- ♦ In what situations does the problem usually occur? What are you feeling, thinking or focusing on when you recognize this need for improvement?

♦ Think about when you were in this situation, and your reaction or performance was at its best. What was going on then? What were you thinking, feeling and focusing on at the time?

♦ What about the times when your response or performance was less than desirable?

♦ What you can do to improve the situation?

♦ How important is this issue to you? How important is it that you improve your reaction or performance?

You've Got to Be Committed

With commitment you can do almost anything. Without it, lofty goals become virtually impossible. The tortoise and the hare was a fable, but it is an excellent lesson in commitment. The hare was a sprinter who took off running fast but tired after a short while. The tortoise was a plodder who kept the pace all race long. He did not get discouraged or give up because the hare was so far ahead. He just kept going at a consistent pace, and, sure enough he finished and won!

In Japan, *kaizen* is a word for constant and never-ending improvement. Not only is it an operating concept for modern Japanese businesses, but it is also a well-ingrained ethic of successful people everywhere. Successful people, no matter how you define success, remain committed to improvement. When considering this concept, questions to ask yourself might include:

♦ How can I make this better?

♦ How can I do this more efficiently?

- ♦ How can I do this more profitably?
- ♦ How can I do this with more passion?

With commitment, we can almost always find success; without it, we are expecting luck to get us where we want to go. Our level of commitment is something that has to be defined on an individual basis. No one can tell us how important something is for us; that is our decision.

> *The degree of success achieved is directly related to one's level of commitment.*

At this point, it makes sense for you to rate your level of commitment regarding a particular goal you have. A rating of 10 indicates that it is the most important thing in your life (high commitment), a 0 reflects that it is not very important at all (low commitment), and a 5 indicates that the level of commitment you feel toward the goal's completion is about average. The higher the level of your commitment, the greater the chances of you actually achieving your goal.

Lowest   Highest

| 0 | 1 | 2 | 3 | 4 | 5 | 6 | 7 | 8 | 9 | 10 |

Committed People Are Disciplined

Commitment linked with discipline. Having discipline is what helps us keep going when we face discouragement or adversity. Discipline is what allows us to not give up, even though we may want to. There is no substitute for commitment. That's why working toward goals that you define is important. If they're our goals, we are much more inclined to work toward them than if they're someone else's goals or expectations for us. If we're doing what we love career-wise, for example, we're much more likely to stay committed, to work harder, and persevere when given setbacks. If it's "just a job," we're less likely to be as committed and to work as hard to overcome setbacks. In a relationship, we're much more committed to someone we think is the one for us — am I right? Commitment helps us to remain enthusiastic and motivated to work hard to achieve our goals.

Baseball is a game that produces many often repeated expressions. One that fits our purposes here is, "We play them one game at a time." Ballplayers do not talk about going on a winning streak in two months. Each game is important, and, many times the difference between ending up in first or second place comes down to one or two wins out of a 162 season. Small but continuous progress over time leads to big results over time. Different actions produce different results. In major league baseball, with 500 at-bats in a season, the difference between hitting .300 and hitting .250 is only 25 more hits. Twenty-five hits does not seem like such a large number; however, the salary for a .300 hitter is generally far greater than that of .250 hitter. During the season, it can be the little differences that add up in the end. It is not possible to slump for the majority of the season and hope to have a terrific late season. By then, it may be too late.

The key is to put forth consistent effort over time. The games in April, May and June are just as important as those in August and September. Concentrate on the present tasks at hand and aspire to make consistent progress toward your dreams. Recognize that unexpected challenges will arise; perseverance and commitment are essential during these periods. It's part of the process.

What Are the Results?

Do you remember when you were growing up and your parents measured you every few months, perhaps keeping track of your height on a wall chart? I believe that many walls in American homes have marks today of the family growth that occurred in those homes. The marks on the wall were a visible indicator of where you stood in relation to the past and also in relation to other siblings or, perhaps, your parents. They were visible signs of progress. Successful people maintain the same kind of records. They plot their progress as a way of indicating their course.

You can't get more by doing less.

Results come from action, nothing else. How many times have we decided we would do more once we saw results? We would work harder once we received a raise; we would put more into our relationships once the other person started putting in more. We would work out more if we lost some weight first. Unfortunately, it does not work that way.

As Brian Tracy says, "We must always pay full price to advance ourselves, and always pay in advance." If, for example, we want to increase our salary, we have to do more. Pulling back our efforts because we are not appreciated is not the answer. If management does not deem us worthy of a salary increase, putting in less effort won't get us what we want. We need to increase our value to our company. When we are more valuable, we can command more. Do more than you are getting paid for.

I have heard the argument: "Well, what if I do more, and they still won't increase my pay?" Let's reflect on that for a second. If you are learning more, refining your skills and improving yourself, is that a negative? If you are becoming more efficient, is that a negative? It may be possible that you are outgrowing your current employer. If you are creating increased value for the company over time and are not being compensated, it may be time to move on. You, however, are moving on with increased skills and knowledge. You have become more valuable. Who has made out better in the deal? The company for a short time may have been underpaying you, but you benefited by learning at the company's expense.

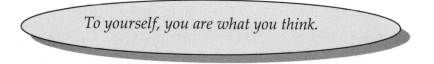

To yourself, you are what you think.

To the world, you are what you produce. People get paid for what they produce — not how long they work at producing it. Increase your salary by increasing your value to the workplace. The more efficient you can be, the sooner you will see that increase. John Maxwell uses the formula, to explain this phenomenon.

$$\text{Quality} + \text{Quantity} + \text{Mental Attitude} = \text{Compensation}$$

One at a Time

Focus on one main goal at a time. Sometimes, we get excited about change. We get pumped up and decide that we are totally going to revamp ourselves "soup to nuts." That may be a great philosophy, but we only have so much energy. If you try to change too much too quickly, you might wind up changing nothing and getting frustrated. Expect that, when you make a change, there may be a temporary drop in efficiency. Don't worry about this; it is your own learning curve at work. Accept it and realize that, in the end, you will be much better off for changing. Start with small changes and build up to larger ones. "We can do anything, but we can't do everything," says Brian Tracy. Decide what is really important to you and go after it!

There is always a market for people who are the best at what they do. You may say, *I am not sure if I can be the very best*. Let me give you some reassuring advice: The market will always accept the top twenty percent. Aim for the top; if you don't make it but have attained that top twenty plateau, you will also do well. The gap between number one and number two is not always large. Many times, it is small increments. The top ten may all be clustered together. Do not picture yourself as moving heaven and earth. You just have to follow the model for whatever it is you want.

Don't be a jack of all trades. If you spread yourself out, you will be adequate at many skills and focused on none. That also means that you will be a master of none. Let your definite purpose lead the way. Do not get bogged down in busywork and routine chores. Do high-priority work first. High priority work is where the payoff is.

Many people swear by the Pareto Principle, otherwise known as the 80/20 rule. In business, eighty percent of your money comes from a core of twenty percent of your customers. Identify where the twenty percent is and go after it. In life, decide what critical twenty percent of your life needs work and focus your effort (eighty percent) on it. Whatever you focus on is magnified, and, if you focus long enough and hard enough, it will grow in importance and in value.

Why Make a Change?

Maxwell Maltz and Bobbe Sommer, in the book, *Psycho-Cybernetics 2000*, discuss the subject of willpower. No amount of will power is of any use unless we really want to give up old habits. Most of the time we'd love to get rid of the painful effects of habits but are not willing to give up the habits themselves. The reason most diets fail after a short time is that dieters start feeling deprived. They have the desire to lose weight, to look and feel better. But the more they think about food, the more conscious they become of it until the desire to eat consumes them.

We shouldn't deceive ourselves that we can change our lives by self-discipline alone. If we really want to lose weight, we must be "sold" on the idea of getting rid of the habit of overeating, which has been serving as compensation for tensions and unfulfilled needs. We will seldom, if ever, stop simply because we think we should. To do this would generate guilt, frustration and anxiety, all of which mount a resistance to change.

As all 12-step programs emphasize, before we can change any habit, we must fully recognize and accept that we have one. If we can't accept our faults and our strengths, there is no reason to think we can overcome them.

Many years ago, when Charles Schwab was president of Bethlehem Steel, he hired Ivy Lee as a consultant. Mr. Schwab was frustrated with his own lack of organization and that of his co-workers. He was sure that, if they could work more efficiently, they could all be more productive. He just didn't know how to go about it. It did not take Mr. Lee very long to come up with a game plan.

First, he asked Mr. Schwab to write down what needed to be done the next day. Then, he asked him to number the items in order of importance. He suggested working at Number One until it was done, then going on to Number Two, etc., without skipping numbers. Anything not completed at the end of the day was to be at the top of the list for the next day. After being convinced that this system worked, Schwab had the management under him try the same process. Needless to say, Mr. Lee made a hefty consulting fee. What are we talking about here? Really nothing more than creating positive business habits and sticking to them.

What Is a Habit, and Why Are We So Afraid to Change?

> *A habit is nothing more than an accepted – often unquestioned - way of doing things.*

When you get dressed in the morning, do you put on both socks and then your shoes, or sock-shoe-sock-shoe? If you have never thought about it before, try paying attention to your pattern the next time you get dressed, purposely breaking your pattern the next day to see how it feels. The change may feel awkward, but that does not mean it is wrong. Habits are patterns and, in themselves, are neither right nor wrong. "It seems, in fact, as though the second half of a man's life is made up of nothing but the habits he has accumulated during the first half," wrote Dostoevsky. A daily routine adhered to over time will become second nature, like driving a car.

Repetition is the key to enforcing a habitual behavior. Habit becomes a part of your life through repetition. In fact, you cannot create or sustain a habit without repetition. Some habits are so simple, and yet we still choose to ignore them. How many people have heard the saying, "An apple a day keeps the doctor away?" Everyone has probably heard of it, but how many people eat an apple a day? What if it is true? You cannot choose to not eat an apple for thirty days and then on day thirty-one eat thirty-one apples. It does not work that way. It is an apple a day. You wouldn't go to the gym for a week and pronounce yourself in shape. It takes time to get the human body in the condition we want. We must continually improve. The repetition creates the connections.

It is easier to create a habit than to change one. Think about it: How many times have you heard that it is easier to do something right the first time? The thinking is the same. If you have to unlearn a habit, it takes longer than just learning it the first time. A habit is made up of, basically, knowledge, skill and desire. The knowledge piece is learning what to do, skill is carrying it out, and desire is wanting to do it. Creating a habit requires work in all three areas.

Habit =
Knowledge + Skill + Desire

What Are You Doing Right Now?

When considering habits, the first step is to identify what you are doing that is habitual. Remember that habits are actions that you engage in over time and that you are not consciously paying much attention to. Not believing in a habit does not mean that it does not exist. For most people, walking is a habit. You do not spend much time thinking about your walking gait as an adult. If you are recovering from an accident or injury, however, your attention to walking is quite focused.

A good habit could be going for a jog after work three days a week. When questioned as to why they do it, people will often respond with an answer like, "I have always done it," or "It's a habit." Bad habits might be something like smoking, drinking or eating in excess. With regard to these examples, you are doing the action to yourself. No one is causing you to partake in these actions. Someone might have helped you get started, but you are running the show at this point. When someone is asked why they smoke, drink too much or overeat, the answers will be very similar to those answers given by those involved in good habits: "I have always done it" or "I have been this way for years." Interestingly, the answers connected with both good and bad habits are almost always identical.

Choice Not Chance

Habits, both positive and negative, happen by choice, not chance. If that is the case, maybe we are onto something. Again, we are not trying to reinvent the wheel. "I have always believed that anybody with a little ability, a little guts and the desire to apply himself can make it," Willie Shoemaker, the Hall of Fame jockey, once said. If you are looking to make a change in a habit, identify what it is you are doing that you are now identifying as negative and in need of change. Each time you replicate an action, it is reinforced in your subconscious mind and becomes easier to repeat. Decide what you have been getting from being involved in this particular habit. This is key to understanding yourself. Be honest - you've been getting some kind of pleasure from this, or you would not do it. Most people don't have cricket eating on their list of habits.

What's the Next Step?

All right, so you have identified a habit that you feel is holding you back from who you want to be and who you are inside yourself. The next step is to identify what you want your new habit to be. It's not enough to want to rid yourself of a negative habit; you must have something else in place. This allows your mind to not race back to the old but, rather, to find a solution with the new correct answer. An example of this process might be quitting smoking. To quit, a smoker has to have come to terms with the fact that the habit is not good for the body. Even so, time will come when the body will call for nicotine. If the old habit has been replaced with something like chewing gum, the process of quitting becomes more bearable. With this or any habit, to just deny yourself because you know you should is a tall order indeed. Why make it that hard on yourself?

> *Research suggests that it takes at least 21 days to change.*

Once you have decided to break a habit, avoid the environment associated with the habit for at least as many days. Again, why place yourself in a situation where it is that much harder for you than it has to be? Many people claim that the biggest obstacle to changing their habits is that they will miss others who also engage in the habit; this is especially true of smokers and drinkers who try to quit. This may, in fact, be true. However, one might ask: If these individuals cannot support your new, more positive, habits, how positive are these people for you overall?

Where Is Your Reward?

You have decided what your old habit was or wasn't giving you and what your new habit will provide. Now is the fun part. **Plan your reward.** Decide how you are going to reinforce your own behavior. When dolphins are trained at Sea World, they receive many fish for their efforts. Decide what your fish will be. At first, reward your decisions related to your new positive habit every time. And plan a bigger reward for when you reach your goal, whatever that may be. Examples of rewards might be something like:

- ◆   a new pair of shoes
- ◆   a massage
- ◆   a romantic candlelit dinner
- ◆   an afternoon just to yourself
- ◆   a vacation to Bermuda

Pay Attention to What Is Reinforced

Never reward an undesired behavior. Many individuals who resolve to make a positive change and actually do can create the wrong reward. Your reward can't be related negatively to making a positive change. What do I mean? When someone says, "As soon as I pay down my credit card debt, I am buying myself a new wardrobe," the reward in itself is linked to the negative habit in the first place. A more suitable reward might be a new shirt or jacket, since these more modest rewards will not require excessive spending. I have known people who have gone on strict diets only to immediately start eating in unhealthy ways when they reached their goal weight. Be aware and do not reward your negative actions. The most important reward you can give yourself is what's called **PRIDE**:

Personal
Responsibility
In
Daily
Effort

What Do You Want?

Write down what you want your new behaviors to be. Most people do not bother to write down an exact description of what they want. At one time, in my lecture work, I distributed worksheets to help people do this, yet less than five percent actually used them. Most people agreed that the idea was a good one but felt that the details were too difficult to imagine. After all, they knew and could remember what they wanted to do. But it's so important to be very specific about what outcome you want and focus on it. Many people carry a list of goals in their wallet or post them in their car or on the refrigerator. The key is to keep them in the front of your mind. How many good-intentioned people make New Year's resolutions and leave them behind by January 31? The odds of someone making a New Year's resolution and actually following through are about ten percent. What happened? They weren't in tune to the process of staying focused on goals for change. People say, "I can remember it." But can they? Can you? How much can you remember of what you read on the first two pages of the previous chapter? Don't worry about it. You can always go back and look. After all, it is written down in black and white.

Forming New Habits

1. Write down the habit you intend to start or to break.
2. Tell other supportive people about your plan. By doing this, you create accountability.
3. Anticipate environmental and other changes in your routine that you will need to make in order to accomplish your goal.
4. If you are breaking an old habit, plan on replacing it with specific alternatives.
5. Write down your intended outcome; keep it with you and visible.
6. Plan on ways of rewarding yourself both in the process and when your goal has been reached.
7. Once you decide to act, the sooner you do so, the more likely you are to follow through.
8. Keep in mind the importance of repetition in habit formation, particularly when you "slip." Be willing to try again!

But the process of creating positive habits must be backed by substance and not just dreams. A thought, when reinforced and repeated, becomes a belief. Our beliefs create our habits, and our habits create our lives.

Accept the fact that you will fail from time to time. "Success is never final; failure is never fatal," legendary Penn State football coach Joe Paterno has said. After all, you are human. You shouldn't expect perfection in others or yourself. Forgive, accept and move forward. Face your deficiencies and acknowledge them. But don't let them master you. It's not wrong to fall off the horse, but it's wrong to never try again.

> *No one can be the best at everything, but everyone can try to be the best.*

Your habits truly identify your actions or inactions and, to a large part, reflect who you are. If you are saying, "No, that's not who I am," then it is time to make some changes. Change your habits to better reflect who you want to be. Keep making changes within yourself until your picture of yourself matches "what you want to see and what you want others to see."

Questions for Self-Assessment

1. Identify two positive habits that you are engaging in. Why are these habits so easy for you?

2. What are you getting from these positive habits?

3. What would you need to do to achieve even more?

4. Identify two negative habits that you are engaging in. Why are these habits so easy for you?

5. What are you getting from these negative habits?

6. What could you use to replace a negative habit and make it a positive?

Action Plan for Habit-Breaking/Habit Forming

1. What's the first step?

2. What research could you do to help you find the first or next step?

3. Whom could you talk to who could help you with this issue?

4. Who do you know who is already achieving this?

5. On a scale of 1-10, how excited are you about this action?

6. What would help you to be more excited about this action?

Chapter

4

Who/What Is Your Big Bad Wolf?

Nothing in life is to be feared, it is only to be understood. Now is the time to understand more, so that we may fear less.
- Marie Curie

A major obstacle to success and achievement is fear. The fear of failure, rejection, poverty, loss or being put on the spot holds many people back from making an effort in the first place. Sometimes, making changes or trying something new or different overcomes us with feelings of fear.

Fear is a natural emotion. Whenever we start a project, take on something new, or put ourselves out there, in an unfamiliar way, we are often afraid. Unfortunately, many people allow fear to stop them from taking the necessary steps (action) to achieve.

Successful people recognize fears but do not allow their fears to stop them.

Can you remember when you learned to drive a car, ride a bike, or maybe even your first date? New experiences can be a little scary because of the uncertainty associated with them, but remember that there is often a positive payoff for trying new things. I recall taking my driver's test as a teenager. I was nervous but realized that passing the test meant increased freedom and a coming of age. As I pulled the car to a stop, the State Trooper administering the test said, "You passed, but you're not a driver yet." I was grateful that he would sign off on my qualifications, but I knew I had to improve. I drove from the testing center in New Jersey to City Hall in Philadelphia, Pennsylvania, located in the middle of a circle with three or fours lanes of traffic going one way around it, with several streets branching off. I figured that this was as busy a traffic pattern as I could find. I drove around City Hall for three hours, and, by the end, I was much more confident with my driving skills. My father wasn't particularly happy when I told him where I had been, but I had conquered my fears and, because of it, was a more comfortable driver. The same is true in all areas of our lives. We are typically rewarded for stretching beyond our comfort zone and facing our fears.

What We Bring to the Table

According to some psychologists, we were born with two fears: the fear of falling and the fear of loud noises. Any other fears develop as a result of our various personal influences and experiences. Learned fears can negatively affect our self-confidence and, in rare instances, become destructive since, when we are afraid, it's difficult to maintain a clear mental attitude and focus. In Napoleon Hill's classic book, *Think and Grow Rich*, the self-help guru focuses on fear as a common mental state that prevents many of us from taking action and performing to our potential. All of us are affected by fear at some level. What's important is that we do not allow fear to immobilize us.

Fear itself is not a negative emotion. In fact, fear at the right time can be lifesaving. If we are in the wrong neighborhood at the wrong time of day, fear would be an appropriate emotion. Fear of swimming in shark-infested waters may save your life. Fear of rattlesnakes may keep you from being bitten. The fear I am referring to is an overwhelming and often irrational fear that we allow to take over our lives and paralyze us from taking action.

Fear is a state of mind. Yet it can be sufficient in destroying our chances of achievement in any undertaking. **FEAR** can also be described as:

**False
Education
Appearing
Real**

It can rear its head in many forms, and the mental image is almost always worse than the actual reality. The key is to know yourself, understand and acknowledge your fears, and then systematically conquer them.

Repetition is key in both instilling and conquering fears.

It would be natural for a child who touches a hot stove repeatedly to become fearful and avoid stoves. A student who has flunked his last three algebra tests might become fearful of taking tests and feel that he is not good in math. An adult who has been fired from several positions in a brief period may be inclined to believe he is unemployable. All of these lessons and fears are acquired through repetition. If the triggering event happened only once, they might not feel the same way. However, the frame of reference becomes strengthened through repetition.

The good news is that, just as repetition reinforces fears, it can be used to overcome them as well. It has often been said, "Do what you fear and fear will retreat." In many instances, individuals who are afraid of snakes or spiders and are repeatedly exposed to these creatures can learn to control their fear. Initially, they might just look at a picture of a snake or spider. Then, perhaps, a real creature is introduced at a significant distance. Over time, the snake or spider can gradually be approached more closely. This culminates in the individual touching the feared creature. When the person can come in contact with it, without experiencing harm and without panicking, the fear is extinguished!

For example, I am not afraid of snakes, but I am not a fan of heights. Perhaps it started for me when I fell out of a tree as a child. Recently, I went through a Project Adventure course, which involves participants standing on top of a telephone pole, rappelling from various heights, and jumping from a 30-foot platform, secured only by a canvas harness. While I still prefer to be on the ground, each challenge I faced enabled me to push through a self-imposed barrier. Which one of your fears is holding you back? What is it that, if conquered, would allow you to take your life in another direction?

Fear of Failing

Fear of failure is the most common fear of all. "Failures are expected by losers, ignored by winners," says Joe Gibbs, who's succeeded in both the NFL and the NASCAR circuit. We fear things such as making a fool out of ourselves, losing our security, going backward instead of moving forward, making the wrong decision, and not being able to live up to a certain standard. When we do not know how to deal with our fears, we may simply stay where we are.

Fear of failure can lead to avoiding failure at all costs. This kind of thinking prevents us from trying, thus keeping us from succeeding. Protecting against a loss is the surest way to lose. How many times have you watched a sports team get a lead only to play it so safe that they deviated from the game plan that got them the lead in the first place?

How many times have you seen someone display the same safe tendencies? After the last stock market crash, many who had lost their investments became so afraid of risk that they only invested in U.S. Treasury notes, guaranteed by the government. There are two problems with this philosophy. First, the interest paid is less than that of inflation (usually 1-3%), so they are actually losing money, especially after paying taxes. Second, the stock market has produced average returns of 8% over the last 80 years. There have been very profitable years as well as disastrous years, but the average is about 8%. Why be so averse to risk when 80 years of history provides this kind of data?

What's Your Perspective on Failure?

Do you . . .

♦ say you're a failure?
♦ think of all the things you should have done in a self-punishing way?
♦ give up when the going gets tough?

Or can you . . .

♦ realize you have learned something you didn't know before?
♦ think about how you will use this new information in the future?
♦ recognize that you know what to do next time?

"Remember, you only have to succeed the last time," according to author and speaker Brian Tracy. Learn to expect roadblocks. Everyone who has achieved success has encountered them; why should you be different? It rains when you are planning a picnic. Your wife doesn't want to move to Florida. You haven't lost the weight you wanted to. These and other issues we face are simply part of life. There will probably never be an extended period when we are completely free from challenges, and that's okay.

If we consider challenges as a part of the process, we become more adept at managing them.

Instead of stopping and not restarting because things become too difficult or fear overcomes us, recognize that the bumps in the road test our resolve.

When a missile is launched from the ground, an airplane, or a ship, it is off-course from the outset. The computer guidance system within the missile constantly corrects for everything from wind to movement of the target to the rotation of the earth. In fact, for the majority of the flight, the missile is off-target. Even so, the most important aspect of its flight is ultimately where it ends. Rather than focusing on how off-target the missile is, consider whether the missile hit the target or missed.

We cannot succeed without failure. We all go through plateaus, with minimal progress and even regression. This is part of the process and should be anticipated. Look to minimize these plateaus, stay positively focused, and keep moving in your goal-driven direction. John Wooden says, "Failure is not fatal, but failure to change might be."

Low achievers concentrate on their failures and reinforce low expectations with negative self-talk. Everything we do to improve our self-esteem will minimize the fears that hold us back. And everything we do to decrease our fears enhances our self-esteem which, in turn, brings us closer to achieving success.

Fear of Succeeding

Many people fear failure, but, for many others, success also creates its own set of fears. Those who fear failure move toward their goals for a period of time and then, as they are on the cusp of really breaking through, they give up. They stop putting in the extra time and effort and start to focus on their past successes.

If we stop communicating the way we know we should when we are on the brink of success, it may be because we become afraid. This happens because we never really see ourselves as obtaining the prize or have been afraid of actually achieving it.

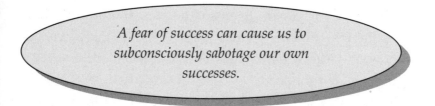

A fear of success can cause us to subconsciously sabotage our own successes.

Why would anyone be fearful of success? Success can force us out of our comfort zone and into unfamiliar territory. Once we become successful, we may feel disconnected or different from our friends, co-workers or even family. Perhaps even financial reward has a negative element — maybe a sense of guilt over whether we really "deserve" it, for instance. We may feel that success carries a burden of responsibility not only for ourselves but for others. I am constantly amazed by the stories of lottery winners who have won millions only to say that they were actually better off before winning — many end up broke again. The windfall they expected to be a great comfort and a sign of success turns into a negative experience. Maybe they just weren't ready, or maybe they thought that money in and of itself could bring them happiness.

Fear of the Unknown

We often fear that which we know least about. Knowledge and action are essential to conquer fear/s. The more we learn about what creates our own fears or what triggers apprehension, the less of a hold they have on us. Fears may be based on a lack of understanding or false assumptions. We tend to fear what we don't understand. Educating ourselves is only part of the solution. Insight into our assumptions is also an integral part of understanding our fears.

For example, if I met someone who was afraid of ants, I would ask, "Why?" Maybe they had been bitten by fire ants years ago and fear all ant bites, knowing that the fire ant's bite really hurts. The first step would be to understand what the person assumes to be true about the ants. Step two would be to confirm the accuracy of the information. I would agree that being bitten by a fire ant can hurt. However, most ants do not bite and certainly not with the fire ant's ferocity. Learning how to distinguish between the two types of ants is an easy way to resolve this fear. By addressing each (assumption and knowledge) separately, we can logically diminish irrational fears.

There is a story of a captured soldier who has to choose between a firing squad or a door marked "unknown horrors." He chooses the firing squad, and, after he dies his captors divulge that behind the marked door lies freedom. The captors also share that no one ever chooses that door. Many people make decisions that they are not happy with because of fear of the unknown.

When you face a challenge with an unknown outcome, taking a look at extremes can sometimes be beneficial. What are the best and worst scenarios you can imagine? Picture your future once these key decisions have been made or actions have been taken. What changes for you? How much fuller/richer is your life as a result of these changes? Now, think about a situation that has caused you fear, and imagine the worst possible scenario that could occur if you make a poor decision or no decision at all. If we visualize the worst possible scenario, often it is not as bad as we imagined, and we realize it's not the end of the world. If we can look at extremes, both good and bad, then reality will likely be somewhere in the middle. And, if we can forecast that our decision will get us somewhere in the middle, it is time for action, not inaction!

Comparison/Competition Breed Fear

If we choose to perpetually compare ourselves to others, we may live in a state of fear. For example, at work we may fear our superiors in the company and view them as more intelligent or fortunate than us. We may fear that those beneath us may catch up to us. When we get caught up in comparing ourselves to others, we are always looking for the next threat. If our family members, neighbors or co-workers become our competitors, it becomes difficult for us to feel good about their success.

"My greatest concern is not whether you have failed, but whether you are content with your failure." - Abraham Lincoln

If we constantly compete with others, it's difficult to escape the hamster wheel. We are always battling others in our minds, instead of challenging ourselves to be our best. This is a battle we can't win. Furthermore, it is wasted energy and, by focusing on circumstances out of our control, takes the focus off what we *can* control.

Ultimately it's about each of us achieving our best not how successful others are. Take stock of where you are now, and make a plan to move forward in measurable increments. We are all works in progress. We will constantly face challenges and adversity on our path to achieving success. Decide what you want, identify a mentor, and prepare to work hard. If you want different results than you have had in the past, try an alternative approach. Wayne Gretzky once said, "You miss one hundred percent of the shots you don't take." Keep trying different approaches until you get what you want.

> *Focus on what you can control, not
> what is out of your control.*

♦ Pursue your dreams and make a meaningful contribution.
♦ Be the best you can be.
♦ Do everything required to excel.
♦ Develop mental and physical links to excellence.
♦ Set clear goals.
♦ Relentlessly pursue your goals.

Novelist William Faulkner said, "Don't bother just to be better than your contemporaries or predecessors. Try to be better than yourself." There will always be someone who is better off, has more financial security, is more well-known, is better looking, or is more popular. Comparing ourselves to others is a losing battle, as it provides and perpetuates excuses for not doing or becoming more. The analogy I like to use is, "No matter how fast you drive on the highway, you are never first." When we get caught up in comparisons, it is with someone we perceive to be better. I haven't met too many people who compare themselves to the people living in Third World countries and say, "Wow, I am really blessed." Instead, we compare ourselves to movie stars or pro athletes or even friends and neighbors who look like they have it all. How many times do we look up to someone only to find out their marriage is falling apart or they are in real financial trouble or they simply are not as we believed them to be?

We are comparing ourselves to what we perceive others to be.

Remember that appearance and reality often not the same. The only person you have to please is yourself.   By comparing yourself to others, you put yourself in a "no win" situation.   What's more, you are comparing yourself to a perception that may be false.

Nothing Is Good Enough

Another fear that negatively affects many people is perfectionism. Perfectionists are typically bright, clever, and successful people who expect nothing less than superhuman performances of themselves.   High standards and high achievement are the positive aspects of perfectionism. Obsessive devotion to perfection, however, can become a serious obstacle to fearless living.

If we become overly concerned with "getting it right," we may never take action. Does this describe you? Is this your approach to life? Do you concentrate on your limitations and failures?   The degree of planning it takes to make anything perfect can be so great that we never get going. Looking back, how many times has the "once-in-a-lifetime opportunity" come along for you? And yet you didn't jump on it because some aspect didn't seem exactly right. Perhaps you did decide to make a decision but learned that you'd missed out because someone else had already taken advantage of the situation. We all need to assess situations and make decisions quickly. The key is recognizing whether or not something is worth putting more effort and energy into - a skill that can be sharpened through self-awareness and experience.

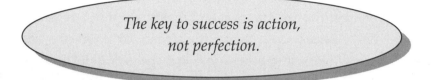

*The key to success is action,
not perfection.*

Success is the ultimate goal. This can't be accomplished effectively, much less pleasurably, if we are terrified of making even a tiny mistake. Perfectionists are generally so averse to making mistakes that they avoid taking action.

Fear in the Workplace

The fear of failure or success can hinder one's career. So, too, can fear of the unknown, or excessive perfectionism. As the name suggests, fear in the workplace is specifically job related. These fears can be so overwhelming that we feel our job, career and/or future is on the line every time we interact at work. Fear can cause people to pass up good opportunities and avoid taking on roles that are challenging; instead, we choose positions that don't utilize our talents, minds or abilities. Feeling overwhelmed can cause us to lose faith in ourselves, and, suddenly our fear and anxiety increases. At that point, even minimally stressful events can feel insurmountable. Circumstances that can trigger career fear include:

- Being promoted to a position of greater responsibility and feeling pressure to live up to the new expectations
- Working in a new department within the company
- The presence of unfamiliar coworkers or a new boss
- Implementation of new technology
- Being assigned to a new geographical location

Size Up Your Fears

When you feel paralyzed by fear, it can be helpful to make a list of all the worries you feel may be affecting you and rank them in order of significance. First on your list should be the fear that has the greatest impact on you, and that is impacting more than one area of your life (relationships, work, etc.). Look at your top three fears and consider the following:

- How does this fear hold me back in life?
- How does this fear help me, or how has it helped me in the past?
- What do I stand to lose by not dealing with or overcoming it?
- What would I gain from eliminating this fear?

In facing these questions myself, I concluded that I was afraid of poverty. I was afraid of being broke, and not being able to provide for myself and my family. I know that this fear originated from my childhood when money was tight. My fear was reinforced as I've been broke at various times in early adulthood. Even when I had ample money, the fear still existed. I had a difficult time enjoying what I had because I was always worried about "down" times. I found it hard to be content and always pushed myself for more. My answer to the first question, "How does this fear hold me back?", was that it caused me to be anxious about taking financial risks. I valued security both in my career and in my personal finances.

Then I went to the second question, "How does this fear help me?" In order to address my fear of financial instability, I developed the habit of working harder and longer. I was ambitious and determined. The fear of poverty pushed me into establishing a strong work ethic.

The third question, "What do I stand to lose by not dealing with this issue", related more to me being challenged and connected with me wanting to do and be more.

In answering the fourth question, "What would be my payoff for overcoming this fear?" I immediately realized that I would be willing to take more risks. I would be more aggressive in my career pursuits and not settle for security or complacency when what I wanted was to really make a difference. My speaking and publishing pursuits would prosper because I could reach a larger audience and make a positive difference in more people's lives. Financially, I would be willing to take risks to create more financial freedom instead of playing it safe by clinging to the security I felt I needed.

By objectively analyzing my biggest fear in this way, I was able to begin the process of eliminating or reducing it and move forward toward my dreams and goals. I did it, and so can you!

Fear and Beliefs

Fear is always tied to beliefs, and how we think and feel determines whether or not fear will rule our lives. Our thoughts have the ability to create our destiny or destroy our dreams. Stated another way, our thoughts have the ability to enable or disable us. We create the interpretations of our experiences by how we feel and think. According to Terry Orlick, in his book *In Pursuit of Excellence*, our thoughts are based upon conscious and unconscious information we have accepted as true. We can develop beliefs about anything if we can find enough data to support it. That's how powerful our thinking is — and how potentially disabling.

Take a moment to decide what three beliefs are limiting you the most. Consider how they are holding you back. How did you come by these beliefs? Are the people from whom you learned them worth imitating? Do you know these beliefs to be true, or have you just accepted them without question? Could you be mistaken in your thought process? Would someone else in similar circumstances come to a similar conclusion?

If you really think about it, are any of these beliefs simply silly or irrational? While all of the previous questions are relevant, the most basic question to ponder is this: **Have these beliefs cost you anything already?**

- Have you sacrificed: relationships, opportunities or personal satisfaction, as a result of your beliefs?
- What is the ultimate cost of not changing your beliefs?

Although you cannot change the past, you are not obligated to continue doing things in the same manner. Some even define insanity as doing the same things over and over again and expecting different results. We are capable of making decisions right now that create a break from our past.

Most things in life are subjective. Our fears must be too, to some extent. There are very few absolute truths. Most of us would agree that opinions are only that and can be altered.

> *Conventional wisdom is nothing more than the prevailing opinion until someone replaces it with a better one.*

The world was flat at one time, remember? How could that be? Today, it is easy for us to disprove the notion. We have more information and thus can make better decisions, yet, even with our increased knowledge and awareness of how subjective most "facts" actually are, we are still prone to accepting others' opinions as facts — and believing them.

We accept or reject information based upon our own personal frame of reference. If an individual wants to believe something, it supersedes reality. It becomes reality, whether it is true or not. How many times have you been in a conversation with someone who is arguing from a standpoint that seems utterly preposterous? Yet, this person wholeheartedly believes this point of view, created with enough self-validation that, at this point, it does not matter whether it is objectively accurate or not. In their minds, they are right.

How many children believe that bad things happen in the dark? My two-year-old fears the big bad wolf coming to get her in her bed at night — regardless of the fact that we live in the city and the nearest wolf outside of a zoo is probably 200 miles away. I can give her numerous reasons why she does not need to be afraid of a wolf showing up at our house. But my logic, although rational, has not minimized her fears, because I am using logic to address an emotional fear. If she believes it, it feels real to her.

How to Identify False Beliefs

To get at the root causes of disempowering fears, try to identify what some of your irrational beliefs might be. Read the following questions and write down your answers.

What situations cause you to become fearful? Do these situations pose an actual threat? What exactly are you feeling? Why do you feel those particular situations are likely to cause you harm?

Do you feel that your success is often out of your control? What is your goal? What prevents you from achieving success?

Do you find yourself blocked by such thoughts as "I can't" or "I'm no good"? What specifically do you tell yourself when those thoughts arise?

List the reasons for these beliefs. Are they objectively true or emotionally based?

Why Negativity?

We all fall victim to negativity from time to time. What matters is that we become conscious of when we are allowing negativity to take over and remember that we have the capacity to address the predominance of negative emotions and the beliefs/thoughts that support them.

Negativity/Pessimism	Affirmative/Optimism
Fear	Love
Hurt	Appreciation
Anger	Curiosity
Frustration	Passion
Disappointment	Confidence
Guilt	Contribution
Loneliness	Flexibility
Depression	Determination
Inadequacy	Challenge

Negativity often accompanies a possibility of failure or the actual experience of failure. We all have setbacks or even fail at one time or another, so it is essential to understand how to respond in a positive manner to this very real experience.

Forget about your failure. Don't dwell on past mistakes.

Anticipate failure. Realize that we all make mistakes.

Intensity - have it in everything you do. Never fail for lack of effort.

Learn from your mistakes. Don't repeat previous errors.

Understand why you failed. Diagnose your mistakes.

Respond - don't react to errors. Responding corrects mistakes; reacting magnifies them.

Elevate your self-concept. It's OK to fail, and everyone does at some point. Now, how are you going to deal with failure?

Whatever we choose to do with our lives, we shouldn't expect instant success. Our resolve is measured by our ability to learn from our mistakes, our courage to face challenges, and our choice in overcoming them. It takes courage, perseverance, and discipline to succeed in any field and in life. Nearly all successful people have doubted themselves at some point and wanted to give up, yet they kept moving forward. And, oddly enough, so many people actually give up within an inch or two of the gold in the seam of the mine. Often in life, we are not rewarded for getting close. We are rewarded for breaking through.

Be cautious, though, about jumping from the task at hand before mastering it. Attempting to tackle too many challenges at once leads to mastery of none. Establish competency at what you are focusing on right now. Reverend Russell Conwell, founder of Temple University in Philadelphia, Pennsylvania, gave his "Acres of Diamonds" speech several thousand times in an effort to generate support to establish the university. The speech focuses on a man who sells his land in Africa to trek across the continent seeking financial prosperity in diamonds. After many years and considerable frustration, he returns to the land he earlier sold, only to find that diamonds had been discovered in the precise area where he had been. What he had searched so hard for, he already had yet unknowingly let it get away. The greener pastures could be right under foot if fertilized properly.

> *Find something you are good at and be willing to work hard at it.*

Fear, Negativity and the Company We Keep

Negativity can be contagious. Our negative thoughts attract negative people and negative experiences. Have you ever noticed that some people appear to have a "black cloud" over them? These are people who find themselves in outrageous situations and to whom bad things just "seem to happen."

Do not allow other people's negative beliefs and attitudes to drag you down. Negativity undermines our self-confidence as we dwell on fears of things that could go wrong. They "burst our bubble" as we celebrate our successes. Worst of all, they color our thinking about ourselves.

Everything you accomplish or fail to accomplish will be the result of the interpersonal relationships you form. We basically learn in one of three ways: through practical experience, by reading, or by association with others. Your ability to form relationships with the right people at the right time at every stage of your life will be a critical determinant in your success. In essence, it is difficult to become successful without the knowledge and support of others.

Don't make life harder than it needs to be; surround yourself with the "right" people for you.

Think about those with whom you associate. Are they generally positive and optimistic, or do they tend to bring you down? Avoid long-term exposure to those who cannot or do not contribute to and support your success.

"I am always longing to be with men more excellent than myself," Charles Lamb wrote. Spending time with optimistic, positive individuals inspires us to become more positive as well. The reverse is also true. If we surround ourselves with pessimistic people, we will be negatively affected.

As an exercise, make a list of all the people (friends, co-workers, associates, neighbors, and family) you spend time with on a regular basis. Next to each name, put a minus (-) for those who drag you down or are negative, and put a plus (+) beside each person who inspires and supports you. As you make decisions about various people, you may see patterns forming. Which type of person do you spend more time with? What can you do to change? Remember, we cannot change others without their desiring to change;

however, we can change our behavior. Stop spending as much time with those you find to be negative or pessimistic influences.

You may not have taken the time to assess your relationships in this manner before, but what do you see? Part of changing a behavior is to become aware of patterns of behavior. Doesn't it make sense that, if we want to feel more positive and energized, we would choose to spend more time with those positive people and less time with negative people?

Negative people are more likely to tell us things can't be done than they are to encourage us. Pay attention to what others are saying, and determine whether you "buy into it" or are making your own decisions about what you can achieve. Most would agree that it is easier to be pessimistic because it is safe. As Dale Carnegie said, "Any fool can criticize, condemn, and complain – and most fools do." It is more challenging and requires more energy to be positive. Being optimistic means taking risks and facing the unknown. Moses Malone, who led the Philadelphia 76ers to an NBA title in the early 80s, is an excellent example of someone who knew how to ignore the naysayers: "I didn't pay attention to the things they said about me. I didn't want to know what they were saying. I figured I was the only one who knew the truth." How many of us can honestly say that about ourselves?

It's important to base our decisions on what we want, our personal goals and desires and not those of others, since, in the end, we are accountable only to ourselves. Stop trying to be someone or something for someone else. Find your success in who and what you want to become, paying attention to your self-talk and eliminating negative thoughts.

If having others believe in us is a prerequisite for success, many of us wouldn't accomplish much.

Attitudes Are Chosen

Just as we can choose whom we want to be with — those who intensify our feelings of negativity and fear, or those who nurture and support our goals and dreams — we can also choose our outlook or mental attitude. My wife is a steadying force for me when I become negative. There have been times in my career when I've seen myself as unfairly victimized and spent time blaming, making excuses and rationalizing. My thoughts at times were something like, "How could this happen to me" or "It's so unfair!" I had to adjust my thinking. Hasn't life been unfair to just about everybody at some point? Haven't hundreds of others faced situations far worse than mine and succeeded? This shift in my thinking has kept me moving forward, and it can do the same for you.

When negative thoughts surface, ask yourself, "What is going on inside?" Try to identify your thoughts and feelings. When you are feeling sorry for yourself or dwelling on the negative, make a conscious effort to disregard these impulses and counter them with positive affirmations. If you consistently do this, it will eventually become an unconscious process. I know that, when I am aware of feeling overwhelmed by negative thoughts, I often pause and say the word "cancel" repeatedly to myself until my mind focuses on something new. It may take five times, it may take ten, but the negativity eventually drifts away and is replaced by more positive thoughts.

If you want to feel secure, do what you already know how to do. Whenever you don't quite know what you are doing, know that you are stretching your comfort zone and growing as a result. Many people seem to accept the status quo and really are not interested in doing what it takes to succeed. They want to be successful, but they want it to come easily. However, it usually doesn't work that way. It takes courage and a willingness to take risks for most of us to take the leap and make a significant and lasting change. There is also ongoing work involved in maintaining the change.

It is much easier to dream about "someday" than it is to make that "someday" a reality and live it on a day-to-day basis. Making "someday" become "now" requires hard work and commitment.

> *"Between saying and doing, many a pair of shoes is worn out."*
> - Old Chinese Proverb

Most people find it easier to live in the hope and daydream of "what if?" rather than making it "what is."

Many believe that positive thinking is unrealistic and that the positive thinker is just a "Pollyanna" trying to escape reality. This is simply not true. Positive thinkers look at problems and try to solve them by taking action. Positive thinking allows us to build on our strengths, overcome our weaknesses, and tolerate our limitations. It helps us focus on the good things in life and allows us to focus our attention and energy on what we can change.

Positive thinking is useless, unless it is followed by positive action.

Take Control by Taking Action

Vince Lombardi said, "A man can be as great as he wants to be. If you believe in yourself and have courage . . . the competitive drive and if you are willing to sacrifice . . . and pay the price for the things that are worthwhile, it can be done." Action is the key to being able to minimize fear and operate outside of your comfort zone. This book is about taking action that will ultimately lead to personal success, however you define it. Remember that, in most cases, fear is linked to failure, but failure is neither fatal nor final. It only has the power that we give it.

No one consciously wants to fail.

Thomas Edison, who claimed to have discovered "ten thousand ways not to make a light bulb," never quit trying and ended with not only a working light bulb but also many other world-changing inventions as well. Finally, many people hold onto negative thinking because it is all they know. Because of the influence of family, friends and personal experiences, they believe that they are not capable or worthy of achieving more. That negativity, although not welcomed, is at least something they are accustomed to, part of the "furniture" within their comfort zone.

To move from the inaction and hopelessness that holds you back, imagine extending your comfort zone in a problem area of your life. Instead of the false security of your old comfort zone, give yourself the security of a workable plan.

Below is an example of the steps you might take in pushing past fears and negative beliefs to controlling your financial situation.

1. *What fear would I like to get rid of?*
   Feeling my financial situation is out of my control.

2. *What negative thoughts do I need to replace?*
   I am not in control of the situation. I'm just no good with money.

3. *The positive memory I'd like to replace it with is:*
   Seeing my financial statement with enough money in savings/checking and retirement to feel secure.

4. *The positive statement I will remember to affirm is:*
   I control my life financially and otherwise.

5. *What images will I focus on to create my new memory?*

I see myself and my family being secure. I will focus on putting away small amounts into my savings account each pay period. I will see myself making the deposits and experience how it feels. I will refrain from using credit cards carelessly and not paying them off at the end of each month. I will have retirement funds directly deposited into my retirement account each month, paying attention to how it feels when I see my net worth increasing.

You Are Not the Event, Unless You Think You Are

Like it or not, at this moment, you are exactly where you want to be. Perhaps you are unhappy. You may have a job that you are unhappy in, a marriage that is deteriorating, a love relationship that is so-so, or a family relationship that is unsatisfactory. Your future may look ominous, but you and you alone have chosen, consciously or unconsciously, to be right where you are. The evidence suggests that you would rather be in this unhappy situation than face the uncertainty of change.

Your immediate natural response might be, "You don't understand — my situation is different," "I'm trapped where I am," or "I want to straighten my life out but . . ." You may indeed be sincere in these contentions, but the fact remains: You have created your present situation and the fears that keep you there.

> *By choosing to allow a person,*
> *circumstance or condition to dictate our*
> *happiness, we abdicate our lives to*
> *something or someone else.*

In effect, we have declared that these factors are more important than our power to change our situation. Our subconscious has adopted the negative affirmations we have developed and, as a result, is delivering exactly what we asked for.

Keep in mind that failure or success is simply an event at a given point in time. How many times have you heard the phrase: Criticize the action — not the person? This applies not only to children but to adults as well. For example, being financially wealthy or poor should not impact your self-concept. If you are doing the best you are capable of or value other areas of your life, such as family or freedom, the money becomes less important.

Don't lose sight of the bigger picture: You can be much more than what you are right now. Keep in mind that we become what we think about most of the time. Successful, positive people have given themselves permission to fail. It has been said, "When one door closes, another opens." The problem is that we often look so long and so regretfully upon the closed door that we do not see the one that has opened for us.

Questions for Self-Assessment

1. Have you programmed yourself for failure rather than success?

2. Is your mental image of yourself positive or negative?

3. Can you identify which fears are holding you back?

4. What do you get out of believing in these fears?

5. What do you have to do to address your fears/problems?

6. What in your life is causing you to give away your inner power?

7. Are you associating with people who support you in an effort to grow or with people who hold you back from changing and growing?

8. Does negative feedback keep you from pursuing your goals rather than serving as constructive criticism?

To Take Control Over a Limiting Belief and Take Action

Think of a problem in your life that you'd like to address, and work through the following questions.

1. *The fear I would like to get rid of is:*

2. *What negative thoughts do I need to cancel?*

3. *The positive experience I'd like to replace it with is:*

4. *The positive statement I will remember to affirm is:*

5. *The images I will focus on to create my new memory are:*

Chapter

5

We Are Always at a Fork in the Road

We know what we are, but not what we may be.
—William Shakespeare

Every decision we make takes us down a path with unique challenges and opportunities. Although there may be several options to consider, we often worry that only one is the right one. As a result, we spend hours trying to decide which one it is. Thinking a situation through is prudent. By weighing the pros and cons, we strive to find the best way to approach any given situation. Overanalyzing, however, can lead to inaction. It's easy to get lost in the details and never get around to doing anything because we are too busy planning for every possible contingency. Life is not easily split into right or wrong, black or white. It's made up of various shades of gray.

> *Don't allow overanalyzing to become an*
> *excuse for inaction – paralysis by analysis.*

With a positive attitude, we can accept failure because we realize that it is part of the process. Those with negative attitudes respond to failure with feelings of hopelessness. Companies, groups or individuals can't succeed with a constantly negative leader. Success in business and in our personal lives requires vision and a persistence, the ability to see the future, the desire and a plan about how to get there - starting now.

How Do I Deal with My Situation?

Plato said, "We can easily forgive a child who is afraid of the dark; the real tragedy is when men are afraid of the light." Remember that events in our lives are only that; we determine whether they are positive or negative. Many of us react to setbacks or loss by becoming upset with ourselves, angry at others or depressed. The sooner we learn to react in positive or constructive ways, the better. A setback can drag us down. Or it can serve as a reminder to focus on the next step, to redirect our energy in a more positive way. Successful people scrutinize the events in their minds, to find lessons to help them in the future. But they do not dwell on the setbacks. They may become disappointed or frustrated at times but have learned to work through setbacks quickly and look for constructive lessons.

Remember, an event is only that until we assign meaning to it. If, indeed, we fail at something, what do we do? We must recognize that a problem exists and seek to rectify the situation. Next, we analyze (but not overanalyze) the situation. Use problems for instruction, not obstruction. Very few challenges are permanent. Instead, think about what you can learn from the difficulty. If nothing comes to mind, remain patient and open to insight.

Significant losses have a way of undermining our self-esteem, which can result in self-doubt, worry or even guilt. Although these thoughts can become overwhelming, do not allow them to take over.

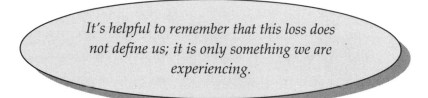

It's helpful to remember that this loss does not define us; it is only something we are experiencing.

We have so many positive qualities within ourselves, and we mean so much more to ourselves and others than this loss does. We can cope with the experience of loss and grow from it. The negative feelings will fade in time. Even though we have lost, we have inevitably gained something as well.

We've Failed — So What?

We all face setbacks at one time or another. It's what we do with those experiences that matters. Don't try to hide from failure; that generally leads to more difficulties.

- Acknowledge that you did your best with the knowledge and skills you possessed at the time.

- Write down anything you learned from the experience (good or bad). If you didn't learn anything from the experience, you are more likely to make the same mistake again. If you indeed learned, write down what you would do differently next time. In this way, we can forge learning experiences from our failures.

♦ Take time to clean up any mess that this experience created. This may sometimes include monetary payout, reparation or, at the very least, apologies.

♦ In reviewing our failures, it is also good to go back and enjoy our successes. It's important to remember that we all have more victories than losses.

♦ Refocus. Incorporate the lessons learned and recommit to the original vision. Keep moving forward toward your dreams and goals. Remember that we all make mistakes and those mistakes are part of the process.

Don't "Should All Over Yourself"

Failure can be especially difficult to bear because, throughout our lives, we repeatedly hear messages about how we "should" act and what we "should" do. We become socialized and conditioned to act in acceptable ways, potentially not even in our own best interest. We feel pressured to live a life doing what others tell us we "should" do. We're told, "Don't rock the boat," "Fit in, be like everyone else," "This is how it should be done," and so on. But being like everyone else may not be where our greatness lies. We can end up not even knowing what we want, much less achieving it. Sometimes, we fear rejection so much that we often go along, just to fit in. We take our place as one of the mindless worker bees, trudging through the same routines, complaining about the same problems, and realizing limited results.   We need to move from our "shoulds" to our genuine wants and desires.   Each of us is unique, and it is up to each of us to find out what makes us happy, what drives us, and how our gifts and talents can best serve ourselves and others.

We Are All "Self-Employed"

It has been said that most people work for someone else. While it may be true that someone else signs our paychecks, in a sense we are all self-employed, because we all are accountable for our actions and the direction of our lives, both in and out of the workplace.   Too many of us act like caretakers of our own lives and not like owners.   Take responsibility; face your fears and indecision.   Perform the action you were destined to make but have avoided for so long.   Think about what you want, not what you don't want or what others want for you.   You have it in you!

"Motivation" is perhaps one of the most misunderstood words in the English language.   Executives often ask me to visit a company to "motivate" their employees.   They are surprised to hear that motivation doesn't come from me. All I can do is hopefully, inspire them to change their awareness, because motivation comes from within.

It is important to have a clear understanding of what motivation is.   Motivation describes our attitude when we would rather do one thing than another at a particular time.

> *We are all motivated in some direction.*
> *Whether we are actively seeking success in*
> *a certain field or just prefer to sit in a*
> *chair. it takes motivation.*

We are all motivated in some direction. Whether we are actively seeking success in a certain field or just prefer to sit in a chair, it takes motivation.

If we didn't want to lounge, we would be motivated to do something else. The fact is, we can't start the slightest activity without having some degree of motivation. What we need to recognize is the difference between positive and negative motivation - the motivation to do something worthwhile and constructive versus the motivation to do something that doesn't result in personal growth or achievement.

Keep in mind that no one can be motivated by someone else. **We are all self-motivated**. We will always do what we would rather do. Every action taken is a response to a personal need or desire that is determined by your present level of awareness.

The Power of Focus

What we believe becomes our reality, good or bad. What and who we ultimately become is determined by our focus and the decisions that result. Do we have a focus or are we content to just cruise along and take each day as it comes? When we are focused, is it in a positive or negative direction? Are we feeling sorry for ourselves because of what we don't have?   Are we focused on what we don't have, or do we appreciate what we have while making efforts to move forward?   Are we focused on learning how to create the results we desire?

Once we decide what we want and what we will not stand for any longer, action is needed.   Get ready to write your own success story!   Know where you are at the present and proceed forward.   Identify your destination and point your ship in that direction.

"Ask and you shall receive.   Seek and you will find; knock and it will be opened to you," the Book of Matthew (7:7).

John Maxwell, in his book, *The Twenty One Irrefutable Laws of Leadership*, discusses the law of attraction: "You are a living magnet and you inevitably attract into your life people and circumstances in harmony with your dominant thoughts."

It all begins in our minds.   Imagination is the picturing power of your mind.   Research suggests that our subconscious responds to pictures and images the same way it does when we experience the actual event.   Our subconscious doesn't think in terms of words, only in pictures.   It may be said that our subconscious is the contractor who will build our life.   We all constantly run a mental movie with ourselves as the star of the show.   These images determine our personal behavior and the kind of life we lead.   We have the power to mentally create a new life for ourselves.   For the most part, whatever we visualize, we can have. The reverse is also true: If we cannot see ourselves with it, we will probably not get it. We need to see ourselves as having achieved our desires. We are all a self-fulfilling prophesy. For the most part, we achieve what we believe we can, and we do not achieve what we believe we cannot.

> *What we are thinking about today is a clear indication of where we will be in the future.*

What we are thinking about today is a clear indication of where we will be in the future.

Successful people are those who can envision what they want in advance. Prior to every new experience, the successful person visualizes previous similar successful experiences. Unsuccessful people, prior to a new event, visualize and focus on past failures. They think about the last time they tried and failed. As a result, they go into the new experience preprogrammed for failure rather than success.

How Does Visualization Work?

When we create a problem, goal or objective for ourselves, our subconscious goes to work trying to find a solution. We can develop an increased awareness. The more we concentrate on it, the more we'll start to find opportunities to accomplish our goals. Did you ever buy something because you really liked it? It doesn't matter whether it's a car, an article of clothing or a house. Did you also notice that, once you bought it, you started seeing more people with what you had just purchased? Why is that? You are more aware because your subconscious has increased your awareness.

Visualize yourself having, doing or being what you want. Feel yourself enjoying this achievement/success. Imagine the details, colors, places and people as vividly as you can. Look at these pictures daily; let them seep into your subconscious. The key to unleashing our vision is to get the feeling that it's working. We must, therefore, picture the end result. Believe that you can get what you want and, even more, that it is already yours.

Mental imagery often starts by simply thinking through our goals, our issues and our desired performances. The more time we take to "be open" and to think about and picture what we want, the more "real" the experience will become. With practice, we will eventually be able to draw on various senses to experience the desires in our mind.

As you practice active visualization, remember that our limiting conscious mind may conspire against us through our intellect. It may tell us that what we desire can't be achieved, that it is impossible. Don't accept this as truth. Instead, remember that we can get what we want when we feel as though we already have it.

In sports, mental imagery is used primarily to help athletes get the most out of training in order to excel in competition. Athletes who make the fastest progress and those who ultimately become the best use performance imagery. They use it as a means of directing what will happen in training and as a way of pre-experiencing their best performances.

Many athletes find it helpful to imagine and feel themselves performing skills perfectly immediately before competitive performances. This process strengthens their confidence by recalling the feeling of a best performance and focuses their full attention on the task at hand. It also serves as a last-minute reminder of the focus and feeling they want to carry into the competition. In other words, visualization can take our minds off thoughts of worry or self-doubt and boost positive self-confidence.

I have utilized a sports-related activity to illustrate the power of focus, yet it works not just in sports but in all areas of life as well.

- ◆ What we focus on, we can make happen.

- ◆ What areas in life have you been focusing on consciously or unconsciously?

- ◆ How could you use this concept to make life more fulfilling and get more of what you want?

Once you have created a direction or a goal for yourself, take time to think about it. See yourself accomplishing your goal. Many individuals who employ this technique reported later that, when they actually accomplished their goal, it was not overly emotional, partially because they had already experienced the event so many times in their minds.

The Four Key Elements of Visualization

There are four parts of visualization to learn in order for visualization to work.

Visualize often. An important ingredient for visualization is frequency or how often we visualize a particular goal. The more frequently we repeat images of ourselves performing and accomplishing our wanted results, the more quickly our subconscious mind will attempt to make it happen.

Visualize at Length. A second key to successful visualization is the duration of the mental image or the length of time that we can hold the picture in our mind. When we deeply relax, with practice, we can often hold a mental picture from between several seconds to several minutes. The longer we can hold the image, the more deeply it will be imprinted onto our subconscious.

Visualize Clearly. The effectiveness of visualization depends on how clear the vision is. There is a direct relationship between how clearly we see our desired goal and how quickly it becomes reality. Many times, when we set a new goal for ourselves, it is vague and fuzzy. However, the more time we spend thinking about, working on and visualizing the goal, the clearer it gets.

Visualize Intensely. This is the amount of emotion we attach to the visual image. As you might recall, beliefs become convictions when strong emotions are attached to thoughts.

The more intensity we can create regarding our goal, the sooner the goal will become clear and the better the chances of it becoming a reality.

Visualization Game Plan

1. Take time to visualize a desired goal or object at least once a day, preferably twice: once in the morning and once before going to sleep.

2. The more you visualize, the clearer and more detailed a picture your mind will create. As you are visualizing, try to pay attention to details rather than the main idea. What colors do you see? What sounds do you hear? What smells accompany the image in your mind?

3. Use actual pictures, sketched or photographed, to help create what the future looks like. Look at these pictures and think about what you could do to make them a reality.

4. Design your goal. Write down every sensory feature it would have if it were perfect in every respect.

Go with the Flow

Healthy, positive visualization leads to focused "real time" actions and performances. Can you think of times in your life when you have been so deeply involved in something that nothing else seemed to matter? The experience consumes you totally, and you lose track of time. It's most likely to occur when you are doing your favorite activity. This totally involved state is called "flow."

Research suggests that the flow experience itself isn't necessarily a time when people are happy. It's a period of deep concentration. Are there conditions that are likely to produce flow? Yes. When people describe flow experiences, they talk about common characteristics in the tasks they were doing. For instance, tasks are usually challenging and require a high level of skill. The tasks are so all-consuming that we have no attention left over to think about anything irrelevant or to worry about problems.

Features of Focused Connection

When you are in a "flow" state, you are:

- Focused on the task at hand.

- Focused on the moment, not on the past or the future.

- Free to think outside the box.

We must learn to "tune out" our distractions, whatever they are. As we become more focused, we are less likely to be distracted. An airplane can be held in place by a small chock if the airplane it isn't already moving. However, if the airplane is already moving and makes contact with the chock, it will be crushed. The same is true with us. Distractions can take us off course if we are not focused. When we are focused, the same events don't seem to derail us.

Focusing Strategies

Find your focus by trying the following:

- Focus on the immediate future — the task that is currently in front of you.

- Reassure yourself that you have prepared and are ready.
- Remind yourself of past successes and recall the feelings associated with them.
- Remember that your goals are realistic and that you want to perform at a level that you are capable of.
- Focus on what you are doing right, not what you are doing wrong.

Timeout

Ironically, being able to focus also means knowing when and how to loosen up and relax. **Sometimes a fork in the road calls for constructive inaction — or action.** Have you ever seen a boat in dry dock? It's where the boat is lifted out of the water for the purpose of repair and cleaning. Over time, debris accumulates on the hull, which has the effect of slowing down the boat due to excess resistance in the water. A well-maintained, clean hull minimizes resistance and allows the boat to work to its maximum. The same is true with people.

It's important for all of us to take time to listen to our inner voices. Some of our most valuable insights come when we are relaxed and mentally open. It may come through formal meditation or informal relaxation — watching the ocean, fishing, listening to music, praying, playing with children and various other forms of relaxation.

Relaxing frees our minds and enables our bodies to perform in their own natural way. We often fail to achieve our best when we are too tight, anxious, and tense or stressed out. Personal bests often occur when mind and body combine for a free-flowing experience.

Experiencing high levels of tension and performing in a relaxed, flowing manner rarely occur concurrently. Developing our ability to relax our bodies and rejuvenate our minds is critical, as it allows us to control our intensity and channel our energy.

Ask and You Shall Receive

Knowing when to think hard and when to allow intuition to guide your decisions is another way to bring more "flow moments" into your life. Our intuition can often provide us with the answers to questions we have. As an example, ask yourself questions that begin with "Who, What, Where, When, and How," such as:

- Should I take this apartment?
- What should I do to increase my savings?
- What can I do to increase sales this year?
- What can I do to guarantee we get this account?
- Should I marry this person?
- How can I achieve my ideal weight?
- What should I do next?

What thoughts come into your head when you ask these questions? These thoughts or impressions can be subtle or fleeting, so take time to capture them. Some people make notes on index cards or journals. Personally, I prefer to use a tape cassette player. How you record your thoughts isn't important; what matters is that you make note of your thoughts, even those that seem irrelevant at the time.

The Skill of Optimism

We have been discussing negativity, fear, and failure, and how they affect our perceptions and inhibit us from taking action. As industrialist Andrew Carnegie once said, "A man can succeed at almost anything for which he has unlimited enthusiasm."

Optimism can be the key to unlock the door to achievement.

Some believe that individuals are either optimistic or pessimistic by nature. I am not convinced that this is true. If personality and disposition are genetic, it implies that they can't be changed. I prefer to believe that we are products of our environment, a collection of our past experiences and the opinions of those we value (e.g., parents, loved ones, friends, etc.). Martin Seligman, in his book, *Learned Optimism*, believes that optimism is actually a skill. If optimism is a skill rather than a genetic ability, it can be learned and improved.

If I work out on a regular basis by running 20 to 30 minutes on a treadmill, my cardiovascular system will become more efficient (Skill). Based on genetic makeup and age, I probably will not compete at an Olympic level (Innate Ability). If I never work out, I will not know my genetic potential (Ability) or my efficiency potential (Skill). While skill and ability are interrelated, without the necessary building blocks (Ability), all the practice in the world won't help! Yet, without the necessary skill improvement, innate ability is never fully utilized.

To teach this concept to young adults, I use the musician Kenny G as an example. I ask if they have heard of him. For many, he doesn't play their type of music, but they do know who he is. I then ask if any of them has the ability to be a better saxophone player than he. They usually all say "no." I then point out that Kenny practiced seven hours a day when he was young to attain his current level of skill proficiency and continues to practice constantly. While he obviously has tremendous innate ability, without practice, his ability would never have been realized.

It is unclear if any of these young people have the ability to play the saxophone as well as Kenny G., since they have not invested similar time and energy. How could they expect the same output (reward)? In fact, in many instances, practice may be more important than ability. The only person who can really say that s/he had less natural ability is the person who practiced the same seven hours a day for years and can't play as well as Kenny G. Everyone else only assumes that his/her abilities and skills are inferior.

> *"How do you get to Carnegie Hall? -*
> *Practice, practice, practice."*

Optimism is built upon having success, the result of being validated by others and by our own positive self-talk. Mohammad Ali said, "I am the greatest. I said that even before I knew I was." In other words, positive self-talk works. Pessimists have negative things happen in their lives that can be traumatic, negative and painful. Surprisingly, similar events also happen to optimists. We all face difficult times, heartache and tragedy. Yet optimists generally handle these challenges better as they tend not to dwell on it or personalize the event but, instead, realize that it is all part of life.

According to Harry Truman, "A pessimist is one who makes difficulties of his opportunities; an optimist is one who makes opportunities out of his difficulties." It is easy to feel good and be positive when everything is going our way, but it's up to us how hard times affect us. People with an optimistic outlook believe in themselves and their abilities. They are clear on and in charge of their goals, thoughts, behaviors, and how they affect others. They choose and take control of their attitude.

Optimistic people expect to succeed.

First they dream, then they plan, then they execute. But they would not have found the impetus to go after their dreams if they had not already expected to be successful.

Of course, a good attitude doesn't guarantee success, but it is part of a winning formula. In some situations, pessimists will be proven right, but optimists will always have a better time along the way! It is also more enjoyable and more uplifting to be around optimistic, positive people.

Life on Life's Terms

Optimists do not necessarily get everything they want, but they are more content with what they get. If we assume that we get what we expect, be it financial, in relationships or career-related. We can typically meet our expectations, whatever they are; therefore, it makes sense to expect more from ourselves. In most cases, we will rise to achieve them, our confidence will build, and success will follow. As we take on a new endeavor, we may lack confidence, as we have no history of success in this area. Still, positive thinking generates more optimistic thoughts and subsequent positive actions.

Our overall outlook, whether optimistic or pessimistic, also dictates how we view others and, in turn impacts the strength and depth of our relationships. If someone whom you value does something that displeases you, how would you explain it to yourself? Was it a misunderstanding, or did they purposely try to offend you? You would probably assume that it was a mistake and that they were not intentionally trying to cause you harm. Now, think of someone with whom you do not have the best relationship. If they acted in the very same way, what would your response be? This suggests that we do not treat everyone in the same way. Do your expectations of people vary? Why is this? What would happen if you changed your expectations?

If we want to be positive, we need to act positive. Enthusiasm drives an optimistic mind to positive action. How would you identify someone as being positive? How does he act? What does she say? What tonality does he speak in? What gestures does she tend to use? If we can identify these aspects, then we can imitate them. Makes sense, right? If we can mimic them, shouldn't we get the same results? If we get the same results, then we are thinking and acting in the same positive way as they are. Real positive motivation comes from within. It is having a constructive optimistic approach to any situation or person.

Signs of a Positive Attitude

1. Commit to staying positive — no matter what happens.
2. Believe in yourself. Believe that you can make the difference. You can control how you feel and what you think.
3. Focus on doing what will help you stay positive and in control.
4. Be willing to see the best in others. Individuals usually meet our expectations, so make them positive.
5. Create a positive state of mind before you take action.
6. See opportunity everywhere. There is always something positive to be seen if you look hard enough and in the right places.
7. When there are problems, focus on the solution rather than the problem — the silver lining, not the cloud.
8. Be persistent. Keep trying your best. Having a positive attitude allows this to happen more easily.

Optimism permeates everything we do and becomes a part of who we are. Optimistic people have more energy and better physical health. The body produces what the mind believes. Optimistic thoughts can impact our entire existence and create a dramatic positive change in our minds and bodies. If, for example, you can vastly improve your financial status, why couldn't you make similar improvements in your physical health by losing weight or building muscle? The key link is the same — optimism and persistence.

Protect Yourself from Negativity

If you are experiencing negative thoughts try some of the following tactics:

1. Commit yourself to stop dwelling on the negatives. Plan to shift to the positive. Pay attention to your own thoughts. Decide for yourself when you are being negative. Decide what action or thought process works for you to shift from negative to positive.

2. Commit to stop revisiting things that went wrong in the past, whether in a performance or relationship. We have all had relationships that did not work out. Decide what you can learn from the experience and move on.

3. If you find yourself slipping back into the negative, stop. Change your surroundings, including the type of people with whom you spend time. Do whatever you need to so that you can stop dwelling on the negative.

4. Find something positive in all experiences. If we look hard enough, we can always find the silver lining.

Prepare Yourself to Be More Positive

- ◆ Stay rested. It is easier to slip into negative thinking when you are tired or fatigued.
- ◆ Find ways to reduce stress in your life. When there is more stress in your life, you are more susceptible to negative shifts in mood.
- ◆ Keep track of the good things that happen each day. Keep a record of what is happening in your life. The more positive elements you can find and appreciate, the less likely you are to be overcome by negativity.

It's All about Attitude

According to author and psychologist Martin Seligman, "The claim that personality is inherited has strong evidence behind it. But, at most, personality is only genetics in part. The degree of heritability hovers below .50 for all personality traits (except IQ, which, may be around .75). And this opens the door for self-improvement." The greatest barriers in our pursuit of success are the psychological barriers we impose on ourselves. Part of having a strong self-concept is having confidence in ourselves and our abilities. Having confidence means trusting in ourselves. Better than anyone, we know ourselves and what is best for us.

In more cases than you might think, it doesn't matter how "good" we are, as long as we believe in ourselves.

Confidence is a belief in yourself even when others question you or your abilities. It means believing in your potential and capacity to overcome obstacles. Becoming successful in any endeavor demands a high level of commitment, a strong focus, and a belief in oneself. "Never stand begging for that which you have the power to earn," Miguel de Cervantes, author of *Don Quixote*, wrote.

Are you prepared for what is to come? Are you focused on the task at hand? Are you pursuing a meaningful goal? Are you putting yourself in situations that give you the greatest chance to positively grow and develop increased confidence? We all improve our self-confidence by overcoming obstacles. We must acknowledge our victories and accept the setbacks, learning from both.

To Increase Confidence:

♦ Act as if you can do whatever you're attempting.
♦ Prepare to do what you need to do.
♦ Believe in yourself.
♦ Take something positive from every experience.
♦ Recall your successes and build upon them.

Life Is a Numbers Game

Since pessimism stems from taking failure or setbacks personally, it's good to remember the old cliché that life is a numbers game. I stumbled on this concept when I was in graduate school and wondered why it took so long to fully understand. The idea is the same for sales as it is for dating, athletics or success at anything. If we try once and fail, our average is zero. If we try ten times and go zero for ten, our average is still zero. If we are zero for twenty, maybe it is time for reflection - maybe it's time to do something else — but it's not time to stop trying.

> *In most endeavors, we don't have to have a high success rate, but we need to have some success. Even a broken clock is right twice a day!*

You are only looking for one person to marry. As an entrepreneur, you only need one really good idea or one way to differentiate yourself from the competition. Think about it; major league baseball players, who make millions of dollars, are only successful approximately 3 out of the 10 times they step up to the plate. They are satisfied with a 70 percent failure rate. Red Sox legend Ted Williams, who was considered by many to be the greatest hitter of all time, failed six out of every ten times in his *best* season.

If you believe in yourself and have the courage of your convictions, you can succeed. You can be optimistic about yourself regardless of the failures you encounter. In sales, you will create a considerable following if you talk to enough people and are not deterred by the large number of non-buyers. If you keep presenting your message to the clients and keep honing your craft, eventually a few people will be convinced and you'll be on your way. Optimism is what helps us to keep going when we feel discouraged.

Pastor Dr. J. A. Holmes said, "Never tell a young person that something cannot be done. God may have been waiting for centuries for somebody ignorant enough of the impossible to do that thing."

Questions for Self-Assessment

1. When you reach the fork in the road, how do you decide which path to take?

2. When you are feeling stressed, what strategies do you use to relax?

3. Of the people you know, who would you rate as an optimist, most of the time? How are they different from you?

4. What would you say is your average ratio of optimism to pessimism (70/30, 60/40, etc)? How could you improve that ratio?

6

Being Ready for Just About Anything

"The future belongs to those who prepare for it."
- Aristotle

How is your current plan working for you? If the answer is "great," the next question might be, could it be better? If the answer is "yes," then it's time to make a change. If you do not have a plan at all, then it is time to make one. Let's start at the beginning. By failing to plan, we plan to fail. Many individuals don't achieve their goals because they didn't really identify them in the first place. How are you going to live the next five or ten years of your life? How will what you do today effect your tomorrow? The goals you set, the people you meet, and the choices you make will have consequences. With planning, you influence what those consequences will be.

You do not have to know the way to know there is a way.

Many of us have expectations, but in reality, most expectations are only vague speculations. Hopes and expectations are not enough; we must have a strategy for ourselves and a plan to get there. The more variables that we can plan for, the more in control we will be. I was recently speaking with a company executive who told me that, for every new plan they implement, they create three to four back-up scenarios. They study every angle, trying to anticipate what might not work out. They do not put all of their eggs in one basket. Who knows what might happen? Doing this allows the company to better accommodate their customers' needs and make immediate changes as needed. "Chance favors the prepared," according to the scientist Louis Pasteur. While there is always uncertainty in life, the degree of uncertainty can be decreased through careful preparation and planning. And, since uncertainty engenders fear, reducing uncertainty may make the difference between action and inaction.

Do Your Homework

If, for example, you were going to buy a new car, how would you prepare? If you are at all like me, you might go to your bank or credit union to see what the recommended selling price is for the vehicle you are interested in. You could do some research, either through reading or Internet pricing. You could check for any pertinent recall information. You could call around to get interest rate quotes for financing. All of this information would be helpful prior to visiting automobile dealerships. Let's consider the downside of not doing this legwork. When we do not do our homework, we have to take it on faith that the salesperson will be honest. But let's face it; salespeople are not in business to give us the best deal. They are in business to sell as many vehicles as they can for as much money as they can. This does not make them dishonest, but they are certainly prepared and intent on reaching *their* goals. It only makes sense for us consumers to do what we need to reach *our* goals.

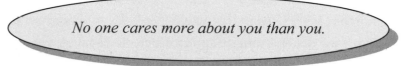

No one cares more about you than you.

Sacrifice Starts Now

"You cannot build a reputation on what you are going to do," Henry Ford once said. **We must commit to taking action in the here and now**. We must be willing to sacrifice the present to succeed in the future. According to college basketball coach Rick Pitino, "Conditioning, fundamentals and teamwork are absolutely critical to success in basketball. Many teams have championship potential." Potential is important, but without being willing to put in the time, hopes and dreams will remain unfulfilled. Not preparing means preparing to fail.

Don't fall in love with potential, yours or someone else's. In sports and in life, it is what we do when no one is looking that really determines the outcome. How often do we hear professional coaches talk about success being the result of efforts during the off-season and training camp? The seeds are sown long before the actual harvest. **We need to take care of the details**. The skills required to perform at our best are developed long before we actually need to use them. The Boy Scout motto, "be prepared," is a keeper.

Prepare to Pay the Price

Determine what price you will have to pay to get what you want. Do your homework. We don't often go to the store and load up our shopping cart without checking the prices on any of the items we put in the cart. If we wouldn't shop for groceries in that manner, why would we deal with other areas of our lives in that way?

Maybe we never thought about it before. Maybe we are not comfortable asking others for their time or advice, afraid that we might be rejected or somehow feel indebted. Maybe it's inconvenient or just plain not fun. There are other ways we would rather spend our time. Maybe it's just hard work, and we would rather it be easier. All of these reasons may have some validity, but they won't help us get what we want or go where we want to be.

Research what others have done to get to where you want to be. Only through seeking the answers will we find them. Maybe, in some instances, you'll find that the price is too great. To quote Michelangelo, "If people knew how hard I have to work to gain my mastery, it wouldn't seem wonderful at all." If we choose not to pay the price, that is okay. At least we made a decision from an informed position with knowledge of the potential gains and costs. For some reason, however, many of us do not take advantage of the resources we have at our disposal. We may not find out the necessary price of making a decision and are left only with a sense of "what if?"

We Make Choices Every Day

According to Tony Jeary, "Your success in life depends upon how you approach the millions of opportunities before you." Opportunities are always available to us; it's just that we don't see them — perhaps because we aren't looking. Jack Nicklaus has said that "most golf tournaments are not so much won by opportunistic play as not lost when opportunity presents itself."

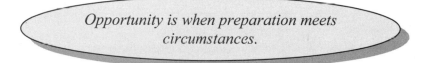

Opportunity is when preparation meets circumstances.

Have you ever noticed how; once you get something, you start to see many other people who have the same thing? Have you ever bought a new jacket and then noticed that there are a number of the same jackets out there on the market? We notice because we are now aware whereas, prior to our purchase, we were not attuned to the same frequency. When we focus, we understand more. When we focus, we inquire more. When we focus, we spend more energy and thereby commit more of ourselves.

When we use a magnifying glass, we can focus the sun's rays to a point that can cause items to burn. The more we sharpen our own focus, the more intent we can become. The more we can enhance our focus, the more we can see through everyday life and find the opportunities that are right for us.

Being Prepared

When opportunities/choices arrive, those who are prepared to make the most of them reap the rewards. It is impossible to sustain a high level of productivity with a low level of planning. We need to understand the difference between efficiency and effectiveness. Efficiency means doing things right; effectiveness is doing the right things. There are two ways to take down a tree. One is with a chainsaw and will take about an hour; the other is with a hammer but will take about a week. Which one makes sense?

Preparing for Obstacles

The following questions may help you to trouble-shoot in advance, anticipating possible obstacles to obtaining something you want. To start, name something you want to acquire or achieve in the next six months.

1. Identify one real and one potential obstacle to your obtaining or reaching your intended goal.

2. What makes the real obstacle an obstacle for you? What are the chances that the potential obstacle will enter the picture in the next six months (be specific about the odds — are they 30:70, 50:50, 40:60?)?

3. Make a column listing the steps that you can take to make the real obstacle less of a factor. Make another column listing the steps you can take to deal with the potential obstacle, should it materialize.

4. Which of the steps in *both* columns do you consider worth taking and within your capacity?

Preparing for Obstacles (cont.)

5. Which of the steps in *both* columns do you consider *not* worth taking and/or *not* within your capacity at this time?

6. What benefits will come from dealing with these obstacles? Do they outweigh the difficulties and costs?

Positive results follow effort. If we put enough quality effort on the front end, we can generally expect good results on the back end. Many times, we have to do what we don't want to do to achieve the end result. Our actions today build toward the future. **Keep in mind the Law of Cause and Effect, which states that everything happens for a reason.** If we can define what we want to happen, we can then trace back through the steps that resulted in the desired action and then engage in those same actions. If this sounds simplistic, that's because it is. Making this happen takes concerted effort. The more we can positively implement the Law of Cause and Effect, the more successful we can be. And the more we practice this, the easier it will become, since increased repetition leads to increased skill level.

September 11, 2001 is a day that many will never forget. Still, as tragic as it was, it potentially could have been much worse. How many of us even knew that the U.S. government had a plan in place to shut down all air traffic in the country? Most of us did not think it possible because we hadn't witnessed it before. After all, why would we need such a plan? Someone at some point decided that, someday, some event might occur when this would be necessary. This is what being prepared is all about. Most of us can deal with situations we see coming; it's the ones we cannot predict that catch us off guard.

We can avoid and even overcome adversity by being prepared. While this statement is basic and dates back thousands of years, it is still relevant today. It is true for military campaigns, sporting events and life issues — starting a family, for instance. We cannot foresee every possible difficulty, but we can slow down or go around as many known bumps as possible.

"There is no substitute for hard work. There will be disappointments, but the harder you work, the luckier you will get."
- Former President Gerald Ford

Organization Is Key

Given the number of NCAA basketball championships he has won, John Wooden is considered the most successful coach in the history of college basketball. Although he has been retired for many years, he is still revered for his knowledge and tactics concerning basketball. He was known for being very prepared. For example, he kept detailed notes about the drills he ran in practice. He compared how he prepared when he won to how he prepared when he lost. Because he was so meticulous, he was able to review his records to see what he had done previously, when his team was in a similar situation. He was so prepared, yet he ran one of the shortest practice sessions in college basketball.   This is most likely because considerable time and energy was put in off the court so that, on the court, no time was wasted.   There was no standing around.   The focus was on the activity at hand — not on the time it took to practice.   Many times, we focus on how long something takes instead of what is actually accomplished.

Attention to Detail

Adherence to minor details is also imperative for success. If we cannot do the little things right, how much faith do we have that the big things will be handled?   Again, to be successful, we must plan to be successful; then we have every right to expect to succeed.

"Before I get in the ring, I have already won or lost it out on the road.   The real part is won or lost somewhere far away from witnesses." - Muhammad Ali

Everything we do has either a positive or negative effect. Success comes down to the ability to handle the pressure of the key moments, to make the correct decision when it is all on the line.   Preparation is the disciplined time spent on mastering the details so that, when it comes to that critical moment, we can handle the pressure with confidence and focus.   As Peter Arnot has put it, "Routines clarify and create order in moments of chaos." Routine preparation enables us to maintain order during times of chaos.

Successful people are like the ant. Ants are always working. Ants don't take days off. They are always in motion. When ants need to cross water, they link themselves together so that others may walk across. They find a way or make a way; they do not give up, and, as a result, they succeed — unlike the lion. This so-called "king of beasts" is certainly a fierce creature; however, he is only fierce when he is hungry. After he has just eaten, the lion will let prey walk past and not stir. He only thinks about his meals one at a time. The ant, on the other hand, is always planning and preparing.

Sometimes, we prefer to do just enough to get by. We are not trying to really get ahead; we just do not want to fall any further behind. We are content to tread water and hope the current pushes us to our destination. This may happen, but wouldn't we have more faith in finding the shore if we were swimming? In fact, it takes as much energy to stay put as it does to go purposefully in an intended direction. The back-and-forth motion of treading water expends almost as much energy as moving forward. Don't fight with yourself; move forward.

"Everything we experience . . . joy or pain, interest or boredom . . . is represented in the mind as information, we can decide what our lives will be like."
- Mihaly Csikzentmihalyi

We must feel good about ourselves before we can feel good about others. You can train your mind to do anything you want. It is impossible to think and not have it affect your physical world in some way, positively or negatively. Every thought or emotion has a physical reaction. Be curious and enthusiastic about learning. Make conscious connections between events and results. How can we make our experiences more useful? What can we learn? How can we make it better? What would we definitely do again? When we ask ourselves these sorts of questions, we consciously connect with our past. In other words, we *value* our past as a learning tool rather than just having the experience with nothing tied to it or, worse, devaluing it altogether.

The Real Victim

A 38 year-old man was at his parents' home for Sunday dinner. He mournfully turned the discussion to his many problems: "I have just left my third failed marriage, I can't hold onto a job, I'm in debt up to my ears and will have to declare personal bankruptcy," he whimpered. "Where did I go wrong?" When things go wrong, it's easy to blame others. Blaming others for our difficulties is the easy way out. Turn on any daytime talk show, and you'll find endless examples of people blaming others for the way their lives have turned out.

Many people adhere to what I call the "Popeye theory": "I am what I am," they say, using that claim to resist change. They do not challenge their actions or motives. They don't ask questions and, as a result, get no real answers.

Unfortunately, this leads to no real progress. They are not taking control of their own situation but, rather, prefer to act as victims of circumstance. They do not control their ship because they refuse to take a turn at the wheel. It is not that they cannot; they just choose not to. This theory is born out of inaction, not action. In theory, we all possess the same potential drive. The difference is that some use more than others do. Keep in mind that your attitude determines your altitude.

What We Expect . . . We Get

Being prepared also means taking control of your expectations. The Pygmalion principle repeatedly suggests that our expectations will be met, good or bad. While we don't always get what we want in life, we do typically get what we expect. "If you expect the worst, you'll never be disappointed. But I think you can reverse that, too," former Philadelphia 76ers president and author Pat Croce has said. It helps for us to first establish expectations, then to raise the bar. For example, a teacher whose students master the curriculum with ease would be remiss to not create new challenges for the students. If individuals usually meet our expectations, it would make sense for us to anticipate the best in others. If we get what we expect and realize what we are looking for, doesn't it make sense to build on that by setting new goals?

Senator Steve Largent said, "You're never as good or as bad as they say you are." At West Point, cadets are expected to succeed. Graduates pass rigorous physical and intellectual challenges, so why wouldn't they succeed?

Conversely, children who are continually reminded of the negative attributes they possess will likely become exactly who we never hoped they would be. Which scenario sounds preferable?

In 1890, the Hollerith tabulating machine was installed in the U. S. Census Bureau. Mr. Hollerith, the inventor, believed that about 550 cards a day could be processed. The workers who used the machine proved him correct; about 550 cards were being processed each day. When the Census Bureau expanded and added 200 new workers, management did not tell the workers that the maximum ceiling was 550 cards. Three days after having been trained on the machine, the new workers averaged 2100 cards a day. When they were aware that the maximum output was 550, the original workers subconsciously set goals based on expectations that were lower than their capabilities. But, as the new workers' performance shows, a limit is only temporary and subjective. Fair but challenging expectations help others to reach their full potential. Be sure that your expectations for yourself are reasonable but challenging as well.

Keep Your Eyes on the Prize

How would you feel if you wrote a book, took it to five publishers, and they all rejected you? What if you took that book to ten more publishers, and they also rejected you? You have now been rejected fifteen times, yet still you press on because you believe in your work. You try eight more publishers for a total of twenty-three. None of them expresses interest. It takes considerable determination to keep going despite those odds. Theodore S. Geisel —

known as "Dr. Seuss" — went on to publish over six million copies of that first book. The twenty-fourth publisher said the magic word, "yes," and the rest is history.

*Persistence and perseverance are critical.
Believe you can do it!*

While unpleasant, to struggle is a sign of growth. Don't misunderstand: struggling for the sake of struggling is not productive. But the strength that comes from overcoming difficulties and challenges is invaluable. Typically, at Thanksgiving in America, families and friends gather to celebrate and to be thankful for what they have. Why do we not also celebrate obstacles and challenges? It's during these periods that the most growth takes place.

At first glance, we would all like to think that everything would be perfect if it just fell into our lap, if we opened our front door and the perfect person was standing there waiting for us, with a large check with many zeros on it to boot! That sounds great in the short term. But in the long run, would we be happy? If it is just given to us, does it carry the same significance?

I once heard a joke about a compulsive gambler who passed away and, when he reached the other side, found himself at a casino with a pile of chips in his pocket. He walked over to the roulette table, placed a bet and won. He continued to win the rest of the day. He could not believe his good fortune. This went on for a week. Every time he bet, he won. He had amassed quite a number of chips, but the thrill of chance diminished. He came to expect that he would win; therefore, no challenge remained. At this point, he decided he had had enough and walked up to one of the casino staff members to complain: "Sir, although I am winning and this is the kind of run I have always dreamed of, I am not enjoying this anymore. I expected more out of heaven." The casino employee turned to him and said, "I would have expected more, too, if I were you. You're not in heaven — this is hell." When we are not presented with challenges, we simply cruise along on autopilot.

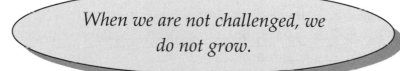

When we are not challenged, we do not grow.

Consider the field of sports. The victory is always savored more favorably if the struggle is with a worthy foe. It is no great accomplishment to defeat an opponent not nearly your equal. Recently, the movie *Miracle*, about the U.S. Olympic hockey team's 1980 victory, came out on VHS/DVD. In watching the movie, I realized that it was the behind-the-scenes hard work and dedication that made the team's Olympic victory seem so much greater. What makes the story so unique is the high level of competition the team faces, paired with the low expectations others have for them. The U.S. team wasn't supposed to win. When they did, they exceeded seemingly everyone's expectations, even their own.

Create SMART Goals

Commit to creating SMART goals. The smarter your goals are, the more focused you will be and the higher the chance of attaining what you want. "SMART" is an acronym for goals that are:

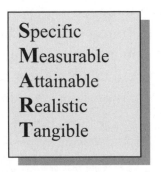

Specific
Measurable
Attainable
Realistic
Tangible

What makes a goal specific? A specific goal has a greater chance of being accomplished than a goal that is more generally stated. It is also helpful to focus on one goal at a time. Allowing for too many alternatives or options can lead to inaction. Identifying one goal at a time does not imply that people should be inflexible or unable to change their goals. The important piece is to have a clearly identifiable objective.

For example, the goal, "get in shape," is very general. A more specific version of this goal might be: "Join a Gold's gym and work out three days a week." To set a specific goal, it can help to answer some "W" questions:

- ◆ **What:** What do I want to accomplish?
- ◆ **Who:** Who is involved?
- ◆ **Where:** Identify a location.
- ◆ **When:** Establish a timeline.

♦ **Why**:   List specific reasons, purpose or benefits of accomplishing a goal.

What makes a goal measurable?   Establish concrete criteria for measuring progress toward the attainment of each goal you set.   When you measure your progress, it helps you stay on track, reach your target dates, and experience the thrill of achievement that spurs you on to continued effort.   To determine if your goal is measurable, ask questions such as:

♦ How much?
♦ How many?
♦ How will I know when it is accomplished?

A measurable goal allows you to see your progress clearly and to quantify results.   For example, "I am going to take on more of a leadership role in the group" may be an ideal, but it lacks a method of measurement.   A more measurable goal might be: "If more than half of the group favors taking action on Project X, then I will move to the next step."

What makes a goal attainable?   When you identify goals that are most important to you, you begin to figure out ways to reach them.   You develop the attitudes, abilities, skills and financial capacity to reach them.   You begin seeing previously overlooked opportunities to bring yourself closer to the achievement of your goals.

You can attain most any goal you set when you plan your steps wisely and establish a time frame that allows you to carry out those steps. Goals that may have seemed far away and out of reach eventually move closer and become attainable, not because your goals shrink, but because you expand to match them. In addition, when you list your goals, you build your self-image. You see yourself as worthy of these goals, and develop the traits and skills that allow you to reach them.

What makes a goal realistic? To be realistic, a goal must represent an objective that you are both willing and able to achieve. A goal can be both high and realistic - you are the only one who can decide how high your goal should be. But be sure that every goal represents substantial progress. A high goal is frequently easier to reach than a low one because a low goal exerts low motivational force. Some of the hardest jobs may actually seem easy when they are a labor of love. For many, being "realistic" means keeping expectations low and even giving up on goals; however, being "realistic" means finding a happy medium between what you want and what you can do.

What makes a goal tangible? A goal is tangible when you can experience it with at least one of your senses - taste, touch, smell, sight or hearing. We've all heard the expressions, "The goal is in sight" or "so close you can taste it," and these are much more than metaphors. When your goal is tangible, or when you link a tangible goal to an intangible goal, you have a better chance of making it specific and measurable, and thus achievable.

Intangible goals are your goals for the internal changes required to reach more tangible goals. They are the personality characteristics and the behavior patterns you must develop to pave the way to success in your career or to reach some other long-term goal. Since intangible goals are vital for improving your effectiveness, give close attention to tangible ways for measuring them. Example: A tangible goal may be to lose 10 pounds. The intangible goal would be the way in which we motivate ourselves to exercise three times a week.

When we make our goals SMART, we paint a clearer picture for ourselves. We are no longer dealing in abstractions (e.g., I would like a better job; I would like to make more sales; I would like to date someone). SMART goals help prepare us to take action, as they provide a map to follow.

Questions for Self-Assessment

1. Are your goals clear, challenging and targeted at being or contributing your best?

2. Are you doing something every day that takes you a step closer to your goals?

3. Is your commitment to quality in training, learning, practice, preparation and performing strong enough to help you reach your goals?

4. Are you doing it because you really want to do it or because someone else wants you to do it?

5. Is this something in which you can find joy and satisfaction?

6. Why do you want to do this?

The Best Dreamers Stay Awake

Nowhere is success and accomplishment more evident than in a person's dreams and goals.

In its most basic sense, dreaming is picturing the future, as you would like to see it unfold. The mind is a powerful instrument, and dreaming is a powerful tool. It is tragic, but many of us are afraid to dream. We rob ourselves of this quintessential human capacity. Maybe we have become so dulled to the life process, perhaps as a result of repeated disappointments that we no longer dare to dream. Whatever the reason, I believe that a life without dreams is a life lost.

I am saddened to hear individuals say they have no dreams but just get by day to day. They seem to have given up but needn't have. Just because something hasn't happened yet doesn't mean it can't or won't happen in the future. As I heard a good friend of mine say, "God's delays are not God's denials."

> *We are never too old or too young to dream or to believe in ourselves and others.*

A Life without Dreams Is Not Living

I find it especially disturbing when I hear children saying that they don't have dreams. Like many of us, they say they feel trapped for a variety of reasons. They come from the wrong neighborhood. They don't have enough money. They are a product of single-parent households. They have abusive parents. They are not smart enough. The reasons go on and on, and, in fact, each of those reasons may have a basis in reality. The journey will probably be more difficult when we start out with personal or family challenges. However, many individuals who have endured similar beginnings have gone on to be successful. Anything is possible, and that is the great part. Refugees are still fleeing Cuba and Haiti on makeshift rafts to get to America, despite all of our problems. Yet many people born here do not take advantage of opportunities available to them. Instead, they choose to focus on what they do not have or have yet to earn.

Dreams Can Be Tools

We all can choose to listen to our inner voice, as it can make all the difference in our lives. We should allow ourselves time and patience when listening to our inner voice. Allow time for wisdom to flow into your conscious mind. Our minds can provide the answers to whatever we dwell on, so we need to be aware of what we choose to focus on.

Examples of empowering questions to ask yourself include:

◆ How could my life be transformed if I did that which I fear?

◆ What in me has attracted these circumstances in my life? How can I learn what I need to learn from them?

◆ What are my most treasured memories?

◆ How can I have fun doing the things I need to do today?

◆ How do I want to feel?

◆ What am I grateful for?

◆ How can I add value to other people's lives?

The list goes on, and we can take it in whatever direction we need and want to. The choice is ours. But, in order to create conditions for the right answers to surface in your mind, it's good to think carefully about the kinds of "bait" you use — the kinds of questions you ask.

We can learn to use our dreams in positive ways. Dreams are not random thoughts passing through our consciousness but, rather, can be a source of inspiration helping us to create a positive vision. Dreams can also connect with specific daily goals. Most importantly, dreams and imagination can speed up our learning process.

Jump-Start Your Dreaming Process

Start with your business and career dreams. Imagine your career five years from now. Use these questions to allow yourself to dream in as much detail and vividness as possible:

♦ What would your profession or job title be?

♦ What would you be doing? What would an average workday be like? What would an extraordinary workday be like?

♦ What would you imagine your workplace surroundings to be? Your office? Your field environment?

♦ Whom would you be working with?

♦ What responsibilities would you have?

♦ What new skills would you possess?

♦ What status would you have in your field?

You can use this type of forward questioning in any aspect of your life. Try, for instance, relating it to your health:

♦ If you were in perfect health five years from now, how would you feel?

♦ What would be your ideal weight be?

♦ What size would you wear?

♦ What would your body fat percentage be?

♦ How much would you exercise each week?

♦ What would your diet be like?

♦ What changes would you need to start today, to get to where you want to be?

Look at your family, and project five years into the future. Think about the following:

♦ What would your family look like?
♦ Whom would you be with? Whom would you no longer be with?
♦ Where would you be living?
♦ Whom will you have a stronger bond with?

You can use this process to examine any area of your life that you wish. Once you think about what you want to see five or ten years into the future, take the time to create a way to get there. What new skills must you master? What new behaviors do you have to start incorporating into your daily habits? What do you have to start doing differently today to make tomorrow different?

Our Perception Is Our Reality

Once we believe that something is true, whether it is or not, we act as if it is. We instinctively seek to collect facts to support the belief, no matter how false it may be. If we accept something that is untrue, all subsequent actions and reactions will be based upon a false belief. Have you ever made a number of decisions based upon faulty beliefs?

So many people never come near reaching their potential because they live under false assumptions. We tend to believe what our parents tell us, what our teachers have taught us, what we have read, and what we pick up from our friends and associates without actually proving anything for ourselves. The majority of people blindly follow the rhetoric of so-called "knowledgeable people" without determining whether the principles of these "experts" are believable or correct. We further limit ourselves by holding these concepts, values and beliefs even after we have evolved beyond them.

"A man becomes what he thinks about most of the time."
- Ralph Waldo Emerson

Many of our perceptions of disappointments have been thrust upon us by well-meaning friends and family members who themselves have not achieved what they themselves are capable of. Yet they offer advice and reasons why you can not achieve your goals. Much like plants, dreams need to be nurtured and cared for to grow. If you do not provide sunlight or water, it would be foolish to expect a plant to survive. If you do not provide a dream with reinforcement and attention, it too will perish. Success is achieved in inches, not miles; it takes hard work and persistence. Some people dream of winning the lottery. While I don't want to discourage any dreams, the odds predict that you are seven times more likely to be hit by lightning than to win the lottery, and those are strong odds. Most people walk out of their homes without giving a second thought to being struck by lightning because the odds are so remote; yet they faithfully feed money into the government coffers for lottery tickets. If financial independence is what your dream is, there are more assured ways of getting there. But they all start with taking your dream seriously enough to *not* leave its actualization to chance.

Change Your Thought Process

♦ Anything you imagine to be true is accepted by your subconscious as true.

♦ Your subconscious can't tell the difference between real and imagined perceptions and events.

♦ Your behavior will follow what you believe to be true.

♦ Your behavior will change when your beliefs change.

Peel the Onion

Woodrow Wilson once said, "All big men are dreamers . . . some of us let these great dreams die, but others nourish and protect them, nurse them through bad days till they bring them to the sunshine and light which comes always to those who sincerely hope their dreams will come true." Dreams reflect thoughts on our radar screen. The thoughts that we constantly think about guide us to some degree. However, we need to go deeper and ask ourselves, *Why*? Why is financial independence so important to you that you think about it all the time? Why is having a relationship so important to you? Why is buying a new car consuming your thoughts? Each of these questions has an answer that is unique to you.

What would financial independence bring you? My guess would be that just having the money is not the real desire. I presume that sitting and counting your money like Scrooge is not what you have in mind. You are probably contemplating what you would buy with the money. I would say you are making progress, but look deeper.

What does buying that shiny new sports car do for a young man? His perception is that, if he has a Corvette convertible, he will be more popular with the ladies and may improve his romantic prospects significantly. I am not putting a value judgment on this, only pointing out a possible line of thought. In this instance, financial independence could lead to a hot car, which could increase the likelihood of dates, and, possibly, to sex with attractive women. That's a pretty strong motivator for many young men. Using this line of thinking, we can continue to peel the onion to find out what drives a particular individual or ourselves. Why is being with this attractive female so appealing? Is it simply for sexual gratification, or is the person trying to satisfy some other, deeper need or desire?

People say, "I want to be happy." That's positive, and it's a start. The real question behind that statement is: What will make us happy? The answer we give may relate to our level of expectation. If just waking up in the morning makes us happy, we will be happy most of the time. If we need to be in a relationship, have total job security, always feel wanted and without life worries, we may constantly be unhappy.

Explore your level of need and assess how much of it you can provide and how much is provided by someone else.

Also, the less we *need* to be happy or content, the more often we will be. Does that make sense? Dream big dreams, but also look inside yourself to find out what the dreams are connected to. In fact, some say happiness is not getting what you want but learning to appreciate what you already have. Maybe your dream is already on the way to being a reality, but you just haven't perceived it that way.

If we can determine what meaning our dreams and desires have and why they are so important, then we can start to really address the issues. Dreaming creates a focus, but the meaning behind the thoughts is the driving force.

Journey into the Personal

For a long time, I defined success in terms of money, but I came to understand that it is not really the money I was after but, rather, the things money could buy. From this understanding, I went on to realize that there was even more to it than my wanting money to buy things: What I really wanted was the feeling of status that I believed things could bring. At one point, I stopped and realized that, in spite of the level of success I had attained, it didn't feel as good as I thought it should. I found myself saying, "Is that all there is?" In contemplating this situation, I realized that things don't make us feel. Our actions and our level of satisfaction are what make us feel, and they are not connected to things or dollars. I came back to the crux of the matter - that our attitudes shape our lives.

A dreamer without a positive belief that the dream can be attained is just a daydreamer. And a positive attitude without a clear dream in mind produces a pleasant person who achieves little. A dream combined with a positive attitude yields unlimited possibilities.

What does it take to succeed? It takes an accurate vision of success and an active commitment to make a journey toward that vision. Success is a journey rather than a fixed destination. We do not arrive and suddenly find that everything is different. The process is what makes everything different. The greater the journey, the more commitment is needed. Think about it: Which will require more commitment to lose ten pounds or fifty? It is all relative, but, in the majority of cases, fifty pounds will take a deeper commitment. Would you take your car to your mechanic if you were planning to drive to a destination only one hundred miles away? Would you take your car to your mechanic if you were planning to drive across the country? Of course you would take that extra step, because, since the journey is longer, more preparation is needed; it is the same with personal commitment.

John Wooden says, "Learn as if you will live forever, live as if you were to die tomorrow." There are two key concepts in Coach Wooden's statement. **First, we must define our dreams and learn what we need in order to go for them. Second, we can savor the wanting as much as the having.** Think of how your birthday was when you were a child. The hope and anticipation of getting the toys we wanted far superseded actually opening the presents. The expectation lasted for days or months. The actual opening and receiving was over in quick order. In many cases, two weeks after our birthday, many of us had moved on, wanted new toys, and didn't even play with the ones we had received. Maybe they broke or maybe they didn't do what we thought they would. Either way, the anticipation is usually much better than the actual experience. The same may be true when we pursue our dreams. The overnight sensation is rare. The hard-working, endlessly improving sensation that is suddenly recognized is more often the case.

I once heard a wealthy man say that, if he lost all his money, it would not be the end of the world because he already knew how to make money. He was confident that he could make it back again by applying the same principles he'd applied the first time around. He was not focused on the end result but on the process. I think that is a pretty strong statement, but the theory is sound. The journey — not the destination — makes us who we are and what we are able to become.

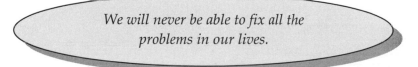

We will never be able to fix all the problems in our lives.

Money, fame or other people will never satisfy all of our needs. In fact, many would argue that money, fame and relationships cause as many problems as they cure. That being the case, since we control our expectations and our viewpoint, what keeps us from creating everything we need? I recently stood with a man at a funeral who was burying his mother. He turned to me and said, "If you have family and health, what else really matters?" This was a grieving man, but I believe that he had the right viewpoint. The baseline for happiness starts with family/friends and health.

All of us at some point or another look around and see others whom we perceive to have it better than we do. That may or may not be the reality. One of the key points of this book is to focus on what you can control, not what you cannot. Maybe someone has more (money, friends or power) than you or a better situation because it fell in their lap, but focusing on their situation will do nothing to improve yours. In fact, spending our time worrying about what we cannot control and feeling sorry for ourselves, takes time and energy away from doing something about what is within our control. Twelve-step programs, such as Alcoholics Anonymous, stress the importance of this in their frequent use of the Serenity Prayer, which is useful to anyone, whether recovering from an addiction or not:

> *God grant me the serenity to accept the things I cannot change, courage to change the things I can, and wisdom to know the difference.*

Part of having a positive attitude includes keeping the focus on what you can control. You can, with effort and practice, control your dreams and your attitudes. Work on building your dreams. Avoid the negative words that function more as dream-breakers than as dream-builders — *Would have . . . Could have . . . Should have . . . Can't . . . Won't . . . Don't.* You'd be surprised how often these negatives can creep into your self-talk and undermine it.

Share Your Dreams with Those Who Support You

Dreams worth living are worth sharing with others. Remember, we cannot succeed without the help of others. Our dreams will take us where we are afraid to go and will require us to do what we are afraid to do. We may need support and guidance along the way, and we can find the support we need if we ask the right people. Individuals innately desire to be associated with causes bigger than themselves. Why not put together a team of supporters — a network — to help you become and achieve what you desire as you help them do the same?

When sharing your dreams with others, be careful to share only with people who will be supportive of you. There are many well-meaning but negative people in the world, and it stands to reason that you know some of them. Share your dreams with people who will support you, not those who will undermine your confidence and bring you down. There are many reasons why friends or relatives could sabotage you. For example, they may not want you expanding beyond them, or they may be comfortable with the way things are now and fearful of how that could change if you and your goals change. The point is that if you feel they do not support your dreams, then share your dreams with someone who can. Changing and growing is not a bad thing. If you do not feel supported by your friends, perhaps it is time to make new connections. Since we cannot change our relatives, it may be time to adjust the amount of time we spend with them and how much we allow them to influence us. Find supporters, not detractors. We can use all the help we can get.

At times, it's difficult to find the support we need simply from family, friends and associates. In some cases, goals require more intensive and expert support. This is when many people decide to hire a coach.

You would never expect an athlete to reach the Olympics or to compete in a professional league without a coach, would you?

Today, the concept of coaching has moved into the business and personal realm. Coaching can be industry specific, or it can be geared toward strengthening your personal accountability. Coaches can be found for guiding and training in specific fields, such as business, sales and sports, as well as for help with specific personal issues — for instance, a coach for help with positive thinking. A coach, or paid mentor, can help you to clarify your vision, goal, and dreams. He or she can support you through your fear, and help you to remain focused, create a specific plan or agenda, and sort through various choices.

Coaching can be delivered privately or in groups. Most often, it's done through regularly scheduled telephone conversations, email correspondence, or personal contact. When the people in your life are too close, or too unspecialized to reasonably help you to carry out your specific dreams, hiring a coach may be just what's needed.

No Limits

Dreaming stems from our mind's freedom to create without limits. Einstein said, "Imagination is more powerful than knowledge." Become more curious. Desire to learn more, do more, be more. Regardless of your level and type of intelligence, curiosity is available in unlimited amounts. It is something every child comes equipped with. Curiosity connects with our sense of wonder, our sense of possibility. What is your curiosity level? Ask yourself the following questions to get a sense of where you are now.

Your curiosity level is	
High if you ...	**Low if you...**
ask a lot of questions	rarely ask questions
like a challenge	like the status quo
ponder over what you read	instantly believe what you read or are told

Curiosity is often discouraged in school, the workplace and even in families. As you develop your dreaming capacity, call the child-like power of curiosity out to play. It will serve you well.

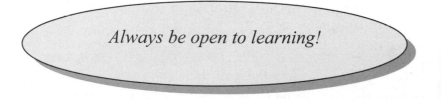

Always be open to learning!

Be Open to Learning

To cultivate your curiosity and make your mind more fertile for dreaming and for change:

1. Cease to automatically defend your personal viewpoints of "right" and "wrong." Defending ingrained ideas too rigidly can make a person unteachable and block the reception of new ideas.

2. Reassess your concepts, values, beliefs, ideals, assumptions, defenses, aggressions, goals, hopes and compulsions.

3. Reorganize and understand your real needs and motivations.

4. Learn to trust your intuition.

5. Observe your mistakes and try to correct them, being aware that therein lie some of the most valuable lessons you'll ever learn.

6. Learn to listen without prejudice and train yourself to listen to what is being said without necessarily believing it.

7. Notice what you are defending most of the time and ask yourself why.

8. Realize that, despite the awkwardness, developing your new awareness will provide you with the means and motivation to change for the better.

Expand Your Horizons

Our ability to dream is related to our ability to expand ourselves. That being said, a vision is a more focused version of dreaming. Dreaming can be vague and all-encompassing. A vision is more narrow and specific. A vision begins with a close look at specific and key aspects of our lives, be they personal or professional. What we can conceive we can achieve. At the same time, positive belief makes a vision even sharper. As best-selling psychologist Wayne Dyer says, "You'll see it when you believe it." Your vision and your belief in it create a new horizon for your self and your actions. It provides a new way of solving problems and is focused on the future. A vision provides inspiration, clarity and commitment.

With a vision, you will not only see yourself pursuing your goals, but also see yourself conquering fears and negativity that stand in the way.

Researchers believe that the subconscious mind can't tell the difference between a real experience and an imagined one. Learn to discipline your thoughts and visualize the things in life that you want. The common phrase, "A picture is worth a thousand words," is true in this respect. When an idea occurs to us, typically it's in picture form, not words. Therefore, picture in your mind having already achieved your objectives. How does the picture feel? What does it look like? What do you see? "To be it, you must see it," according to motivational speaker and author Les Brown. The more you visualize (run the tape in your mind), the more believable it will become to you. Repeat this process daily, as repetition establishes a stronger pattern.

As you begin to pay attention to your big dreams and focused visions, talk with yourself, providing important "captions" to the pictures you're forming in your mind. Some questions to ask yourself are: Do I really want this? Is what I want right, according to my value system? Is what I want realistic? Can I clearly visualize what I want? What parts are fuzzy?

Imagination is not just the tool of the artist. It is the tool for success in every field. As it turns out, the best way to be awake is to be awake to your dreams — and to bring them, vision by vision, to life.

Questions for Self-Assessment

1. What do you dream about (both waking and sleeping)?

2. Do you look for answers to questions in your dreams?

3. Why are your dreams important to you?

4. With whom do you share your dreams?

Chapter
8

Determining Our Destination

"If a man does not know what port he is steering for,
no wind is favorable"
- Seneca

Goal-setting is something that all of us understand at some level, although most do not understand fully. If you asked a four-year-old what he wanted for his birthday, he would easily rattle off his "goals," which would, of course, be the toys he most wanted. You could ask the same boy, at age ten, what he wanted to be when he grew up, and the "goal," again, would be "clear" — he might answer that he wanted to be an astronaut or sports figure. Yet when we see that same boy as man, he may not be able to provide a definitive answer to the same questions.

If we don't know what we want, we are never going to get it. In many ways, as we become adults, we become less able to dream and set our own goals because we get locked into our daily lives with adult responsibilities and significant time constraints.   Society teaches us to find our place, get comfortable, and stay there.

In the workshops, seminars, and classes I've taught on goal-setting, there are always a few who not only have set goals but can also rattle them off without hesitation. Unfortunately, for the vast majority of students I've worked with, this is not the case.   Some claim to have set goals but don't remember what they are (I'm sure they are making great progress); others say that they've tried to set goals in the past but found it didn't work or didn't seem important.

Some people have vague dreams that they refer to as goals and some people simply refuse to set goals because of possible failure or rejection.

I've dealt with frustrated students who have come to me and said that they can't seem to have success in the classroom.   Many of these students have long-term goals (they want to get a good grade).   The issue that many of them run into is that they have a hard time creating workable short-term goals.   They never have time to study or don't really understand the concepts but don't want to ask.   Then they struggle on exams or projects and wonder why.   Like all of us in life, they need to learn that having long-term success is linked to having many short-term successes.

Goal-setting means taking responsibility for the steps toward the goal and learning to change.   In the above students' cases, I don't believe it was the goals that were faulty; rather, it was the resolve to take the necessary steps to achieve them that was lacking.

> "'Would you tell me please, which way I ought to go from
> here?' said Alice.
> 'That depends a good deal on where you want to get to,'
> said the Cat.
> 'I don't much care where,' said Alice.
> 'Then it doesn't matter which way you go,' said the Cat."
> - Lewis Carroll, *Alice's Adventures in Wonderland*

While dreaming and goal-setting are both necessary ingredients for success, they are not the same thing. Anyone can dream. Dreaming is easy and fun. When I scuba dive, I dream that I will find a treasure worth millions of dollars. In reality, the chances of this happening are very remote. If it were to happen, it would be the result of luck, not of something I did. If I were actively researching pirates and lost ships, my odds might be better, but realizing my dream would still be unlikely. I might spend thousands of dollars and hire a crew to drag a sonar buoy for alerting me of anomalies on the bottom — which would be more like goal-setting. But, since I am not going to spend the time or money to make this happen, I must accept my remote chance and continue to dream that one day I may find something.

Dreaming can be amusing, but it doesn't involve any additional effort. We can all dream about finances, relationships, recreation — you name it.

The difference between dreaming and goal-setting is that goal-setting provides the map of how to get to our dreams.

Many people, through experience, have learned *not* to dream. It's risky, and we may be disappointed. That is true. We can't be assured that all of our dreams will come true. However, if we have no dreams to motivate us, can we ever be truly happy? Having no real dreams or aspirations leads to feelings of hopelessness and dysfunction. How could it not? It would be like getting in your car, putting it in neutral, and just idling. Sure, you could say that, in neutral, you're not going backwards. But you aren't going forward, either. And what if the car you are sitting in is a Porsche or Jaguar? Wouldn't it be a shame to waste a great car like that just idling? Isn't it a shame when we waste our own potential and great opportunities doing the same?

Chart Your Course

What is happening in your life today? What do you want out of life? How do you define success in your family life? Your health? Your financial and professional life? What does it mean to be a successful contributor to your community? What would it mean to succeed spiritually, socially or mentally?

In thinking about these dreams and ideals, people often end up focusing on what they don't have. Yet, if we are constantly seeking what we don't have, can we ever be happy? We need to find a level of contentedness with what we do have because there will always be items or objectives whose attainment is impossible or out of our control.

But wait a minute — if we are talking about goal-setting, why suggest settling for what we have or what is relatively attainable? There is a subtle nuance here. I do believe that we can be happy with what we have, who we are, and what we have accomplished. At the same time, I believe that we are all capable of attaining more than we currently have. The key is to enjoy the journey while also moving forward. Goals are necessary stepping stones to help us cross the river of life.

> *Goals relate to our internal sense of purpose.*

In our fast-paced world, it is easy to get so caught up in the daily grind that we fail to focus on self-improvement. Goals help us develop and define priorities. Goals help us to understand the difference between short-term and long-term gratification. As Charles Noble said, "You must have long-range goals to keep you from being frustrated by short-range failures." Goals help us become focused on the present, while dreaming of the future. Goals are our markers for improvement; they chart our progress. This is one of the reasons to write down goals. If we don't write them down, they can become unclear or "fuzzy." When they are written down, we can refer to them to evaluate what we have accomplished and what we need to work on. In short, writing down goals makes them more real.

From Dream to Goal: The Groundwork

I have adapted this questionnaire from an associate of mine. Take the time to look it over and see how it relates to you. Write your goal, and then answer the questions with the answers that come to mind. Take time to connect with yourself and to be as honest as you can about your motivations.

My Goal: _____

1. **Why do I really want to achieve this goal?**
   Prestige   Credibility
   More money   Personal growth
   Self-satisfaction   To prove something to
   Other _____   someone else

2. **How might making the changes needed to reach the goal affect me adversely?**
   Threaten my spouse or significant other
   Upset the status quo of my family
   Compromise my principles
   Compromise my privacy
   Alienate my friends
   Take up all my time
   Require a greater commitment (of time/of money) on my part
   Other _____

3. **How might *not* pursuing this goal affect me adversely?**
   Set me back in my career / personal life
   Limit me financially
   Make me feel like a failure
   Other _____

4. **What am I unwilling to do to achieve these changes?**
   To accept added responsibilities
   To discipline myself
   Unwilling to _____

> **5. How could I make myself more open to these changes?**
> Openly discuss my fears with family, friends or others whom
>   I trust
> Consider my action plan an investment
> Consider what will happen if I do not change
> Consider what the best possible result of this change would be
> Consider what the worst possible result of this change would be
>
> Evaluate your answers to determine your own reasons for
> procrastinating on this stated goal. For example, if you are hoping to
> lose weight because you want to be more attractive to others,
> perhaps you haven't yet done so because that isn't as strong a
> motivation as wanting to be healthy and comfortable for yourself.

Identify Your Major Definite Purpose

In order to give your dreams and goals shape and greater
meaning, it helps to identify your major definite purpose.
Identifying your major purpose transcends any form of goal-
setting. Goals are simply stepping stones on the path of life.
Your major definite purpose is the path itself. Having a
purpose in life does not mean that everything will go your
way. However, it does make the challenges appear more
meaningful and approachable. As Nietzsche wrote, "He
who has a why can bear almost any how."

*You can have almost anything in life if you
are definite about it.*

Most of the time, we are far too vague in identifying what
we want. Thus, many of our goals die in the realm of
wishful thinking. People often say to me, "I don't really
know what I want." It's okay to not know exactly what you

want, but it's not okay to stop looking. When we decide to stop thinking about our purpose, we subconsciously settle for someone else's roles, expectations and plans for us.

> *Not to decide is to decide, since choice is inevitable.*

Not to choose success is equivalent to choosing failure. We all know what we *should* be doing, but, instead we often settle for indecision and feelings of self-doubt and inadequacy.

A Major Definite Purpose

To help identify your major definite purpose, think of something that you love to do or something that you would love to do.

- ◆ If you could, you would do it without pay.
- ◆ You do it well.
- ◆ You have had success doing it or something related to it already in life.
- ◆ It was easy for you to learn.
- ◆ It holds your attention.
- ◆ You are interested in it.
- ◆ When you are involved in it, time stands still.

Thinking about your major definite purpose is about seeing your life in "the bigger picture." Decide who you want to be and what you want to do with your life. If you were to die tomorrow, what legacy would you have left behind? Whom would have been positively affected by knowing you? It's important to identify things that are most meaningful to you. Explore your options. Investigate your passion. Decide what you want to achieve in your life. Create a plan for accomplishing it, and stick to it.

Write down, in a couple of sentences, what you or your business is all about. If you cannot explain yourself in that short of a span, you are not yet as focused as you can become. If you can clearly describe your definite purpose, you are on your way. Tell others what your definite purpose is. This establishes accountability. Remember, when we are accountable to others, we need to assume that they are always looking. Act as if everyone sees everything and everything counts because we never know who is looking at any given time. When we are acting in ways that support our definite purpose, we are strengthening our resolve. When we act in ways that are contrary to our identified purpose, we weaken our vision, both in our eyes and the eyes of others.

Tap into your major definite purpose, and your dreams and goals will have a "North Star" to follow. Start by considering these questions:

- ◆ What is the most exciting thing you have done in your life?

- ◆ What is the most vivid positive emotional experience of the past five years?

- ◆ Why does that experience stand out in your mind?

- How could you create similar experiences and challenges to reproduce those feelings?
- Make a point at the end of each day to reflect on what was the best part of the day. What made it so?

This will be your starting point for identifying what you really like to do. Once you have identified what you like to do, find ways to spend more time doing those things.

Focus Your Search; Develop a Plan

Once you are clear about your major definite purpose and your dreams, your goals should be personal and as specific as you can make them. They should be centered on what you can control and not related to the behaviors of others. I have a dear friend who constantly drinks too much. It can't be my goal that he stop drinking because I am not in control of his situation. Many times, psychologists counseling couples hear statements such as, "If he would only . . ." or "She should know . . ." In reality, the only person we can change is ourselves, which is why the only person we can set goals for is ourselves. We can have dreams for others, but, remember dreams are really only wishes, not reasonable expectations.

Set goals that are achievable but not out of sight.

When I am work with young men, I typically ask them how much weight they can bench press for one repetition.

Often, many do not know, but the answer is typically 150–250 pounds. If an individual can bench press 250 pounds, I will ask if he can bench 400 pounds. He usually will reply with a "no." I then state it another way. I ask him how he knows that he cannot lift that much. The answer is typically because he hasn't been able to do it so far. I've asked athletes like this if their answer would still be "no" if I offered the right dollar figure and a year to train. For some of them, it is. They just can't see it as a goal because it is too far out of sight. But for others, I have just provided them with the appropriate stimulus and a fair timeframe.

Give yourself the right stimuli and fair parameters for meeting your goals, too. Develop a plan for your goals. Get as specific as possible. What is required for you to meet your goals? Whose help will you need to make it work? The more focused you can become, the more clear the picture will be.

Think of using a microscope; if you do not focus the lens, it really does not matter have how good the equipment is.

If you are looking for financial security, determine exactly how much money it will take for you to feel financially secure. If you are looking for a relationship, determine what qualities are important in a person. Break down your goal into small parts. It will be easier to determine what you really are working towards.

How High Should I Reach?

Most who study, write on and lead seminars on goal-setting feel that it is wise to set quantifiable goals anywhere between twenty and forty percent higher than current level. This is their level of essential tension, at which there is a 50/50 chance of succeeding. This creates a sense of challenge. At this point, the goal is in the distance, but it is not so far away that it is believed to be out of reach. Research indicates that people who believe that a goal is out of reach will not try because they view the goal as beyond them. Equally, as certain goals approach your reach, new ones can be set to keep the "essential tension" factor in play.

What's more, each time a goal is attained; it is easier to go after the next.

Pat Croce says that "arriving at one goal is the starting point of another." For instance, with our young daughter, my wife and I make a big deal when she meets goals like going to the bathroom, finding shoes and picking up toys. As she masters these simple tasks, we step up the level and complexity of our goals for her. As adults, we do this without a second thought — or do we? Once a goal is attained, it no longer fosters growth and development. That is why we must constantly assess and change our goals. Achieving goals can provide an energy impetus to drive us to levels we have never dreamed of.

Make your goals along the way manageable. It is hard to know if you are winning when you do not keep score.

Construct a plan and keep a record. If you can measure it, you can manage it. Keep in mind that goals are dreams with deadlines. Realistic timelines are needed. If someone were sixty pounds overweight and wanted to lose weight, it would be unrealistic to expect to lose that much weight in a month or two. Certainly, concentrated good nutrition and exercise choices over a period of time can be expected to lead to significant weight loss, but the timeline must be realistic.

Commit to ongoing learning. As you move toward the goals that you have set, changes begin to happen. Don't be content to get to the plateau. To continue to grow, it's good to reflect on what you have done well, assess your performance, and identify areas for further improvement.

Remind yourself constantly of your plan. Write down your plan.   Read your plan, at least twice a day. Affirmations are important. In and of themselves, they will not make the difference, but they can help to counteract the negative tapes that we play about ourselves in our own minds. I know individuals who post notes for themselves in the bathroom, on their refrigerator and in their car. They constantly remind themselves of their goals and keep them at the forefront of everything they do.   They remind themselves without consciously having to think about reminding themselves. If we can believe it, we can achieve it.

Self Suggestions

- ◆   I am capable of achieving my goals.
- ◆   I choose my future.
- ◆   I choose to be successful.
- ◆   I learn from setbacks and move forward.
- ◆   I am in control of myself.

The Present Doesn't Need to Be the Future

If you are being honest, you are probably not where you want to be in all areas of your life, doing what you want to do and with the people with whom you want to do it. For every goal, you need a starting point. By being honest with yourself and preparing yourself to overcome any obstacles that lie ahead, you can put yourself on the path that is right for you.

We've all heard more than one story about people who started with less yet achieved more. All you need to do is follow their path. That is why mentoring is so important. You do not have to reinvent the wheel for every goal that you have. If you want to be a better cook, what would you do? You would talk with people who are better cooks, buy a variety of cookbooks, and try out different recipes. You would not go into your kitchen, declare that you want to be a better cook, and then start indiscriminately combining ingredients. It would take forever to make marked progress that way. Take the action step; pick a destination — and a path — that is right for you!

"What you do, where you go, and what you become depends on your willingness to work toward a goal."
- Former President Ronald Reagan

What are your greatest abilities and liabilities? Identify your strengths and limitations. What are your most significant personal and professional goals for the next six months? What is your major personal and professional goal for next year? Where do you see yourself in five years, twenty years? Twenty years from now, where will you be living, what will you be doing, and who will you be doing it with? What will your health be like? How about your financial situation? If you're not satisfied with where you are at present — and even if you are — think about the future in ways that allow it to truly become your present.

As with everything we have talked about thus far, goal-setting is a process; there are certain steps in the process that are common to many who have sought and attained success.

> *Identify the goal that you want to set*
> *in a specific area of your life.*
> *Next, write it down.*

Remember, when your goals are on paper, it is more difficult to ignore or disregard them. You become accountable to yourself. Writing also helps us to clarify our thoughts. Often, what we think is clear in our head may not be as clear when expressed verbally. How many times have you heard someone say, "You know what I mean" when you really *didn't* know? How many times have you struggled to express yourself, yet it didn't come out the way you had planned? This is why writing down your goals is so important. Make it clear for yourself.

Tips for Writing Down Goals

How you write down your goals can make a big difference in whether or not you attain them.

♦ Stating your goals in the present tense, or telling yourself the truth in advance, is considered to be more effective than doing so in the future tense.

> Future tense – *I will quit smoking*.
> Present tense – *I am healthy and smoke-free*.

♦ Positively stated goals are often more effective than negatively stated ones.

> Negatively stated – *I do not yell at my spouse*.
> Positively stated – *My spouse and I have great communication*.

♦ Pick one area of your life at a time (financial, romantic, professional, spiritual, etc.).

♦ As much as possible, try to list specific, measurable and obtainable goals.

♦ Keep your goals focused on what *you* can do, using the first person ("I" statements) rather than the third person ("he," she," "it," or "they" statements).

> Third Person - *My staff will respect me more*.
> First person – *I am in control of my life*.

♦ Don't forget to write down how you will reward yourself for approaching and reaching your goal.

The Past Does Not Equal the Future

Just because someone else hasn't accomplished your goal does not mean you can't accomplish it. If you know what you want to accomplish, that is what you need to focus on. For years, it was a "known fact" that a human could not run a mile in under four minutes. This was accepted because it had not been done. The logic was that so many athletes had tried and failed that it had to be impossible. Then, along came Roger Banister, who broke through the four-minute barrier. Amazingly, in the months that followed, a number of sprinters broke the record as well. Did everyone suddenly become faster, or were they all being held back by their subconscious mind until Banister broke the record? Given that the subconscious mind supports what the conscious minds believes to be truth, did their subconscious minds suddenly empower them to believe that they, too, could run a mile in under four minutes?

No matter how many books we have read or how many training programs we attend, we can always make personal improvements that lead to growth and learning. Professionals in every field know this. Athletes constantly experiment, try new techniques, strive for an edge over their competition. Through growth and learning, we can unhinge ourselves from past beliefs and experiences that keep our conscious and unconscious minds from moving forward.

"The man who graduates today and stops learning tomorrow is uneducated the day after,"- Newton Baker

Once we complete our formal training or education, it is easy to forget how to learn. We forget how difficult learning can be and how hard we have to work. We forget the good stuff, too — the thrill and excitement of mastering something new and accomplishing something we couldn't do before.

Learn from past successes and failures, but do not rely exclusively on the past as your model for what the future holds. While the past brings experience and wisdom, the future is where you can apply that knowledge. What we do today determines what we'll be tomorrow. Who you were does not have to be who you are or who you become. You can change your future at any point — why not now? In the words of Mark Twain, letting the past limit your future has its drawbacks: "One should be careful to get out of an experience only the wisdom that is in it, and stop there; lest we be like the cat that sat down on a hot stove lid! She will never sit down on a hot stove lid again, and that's well; but also she will never sit down on a cold one either."

Pay Me Now or Pay Me Later

We have the right and option to choose anything we want to do — anything at all. We have the free will to do anything we wish within the limits of our intellectual and physical capabilities. We are allowed to make mistakes, fail, lie, cheat, cry or shout; be lazy, angry, selfish, loyal, or aggressive; overindulge in food, drink or sex; we are also allowed to change our minds or do anything else we want.

Freedom to choose goes hand-in-hand with responsibility.

The individual choice is ours, but free will does not guarantee that we make the "right" choice all the time! The more freedom we want for ourselves, the more responsibility we need to accept.   There is a price for everything in life. While you contemplate the benefits of making changes in your life, also consider what the potential costs will be.   Writer Robert Lewis Stevenson said, "Everybody, sooner or later, sits down to a banquet of consequences." There is a cost for taking action and also for inaction. Creating a more physically fit body takes time and energy.   Having financial security in the future is created through sacrifice in the present. Earning a college degree means less money now as well as less free time. We all should consider the consequences regarding the changes we are considering making as we hone our dreams into real goals.

We all possess different assets and liabilities — these come under scrutiny when we're considering the costs and consequences of pursuing (or not pursuing) our goals. The biggest price to pay is commitment. To move forward in a timely fashion, we must develop a level of commitment. Those who are successful are more like you than you may think. They get nervous. They experience ups and downs. What separates the successful from the unsuccessful is their level of commitment, especially when things are not going as planned. Sometimes, all we have left is our commitment. Sometimes, we have walked too far down the road to consider walking back and starting over. It is during these times that our commitment and resolve are tested. If you believe in yourself and have the passion of your convictions, you can succeed. You will find a way. As the playwright George Bernard Shaw said, "People are always blaming their circumstances for what they are. I don't believe in circumstances. The people who get on in this world are the people who get up and look for the circumstances they want, and if they can't find them, make them."

Pursue your goals and make a meaningful contribution. Do everything needed to excel in your area of focus. Dedicate yourself each day to doing something that brings you closer to your goals. A goal does not have to be the only thing in your life, but it needs to be your only focus while you are engaged in the steps leading to its attainment.

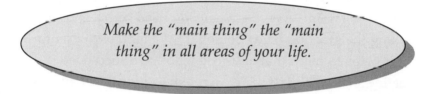

Make the "main thing" the "main thing" in all areas of your life.

With a strong commitment, you can meet your goals and find your success.

There is a story of a gentleman having a prize-winning garden. This was a garden that took many years to cultivate and was created from a rocky, overgrown lot. When the judges came to view the garden, one commented on how nice the garden looked, especially since she was familiar with the way the lot had looked previously. The gardener thanked her and claimed that he and God had created a very attractive garden. Another judge remarked that, without God, the gardener would have had little success. The gardener replied, "That is certainly true, but you should have seen it when God had it all by himself." When we work hard, it is amazing how many things work out. "It has been my observation that most successful people get ahead during the time other people waste," Henry Ford said. Commitment is the willingness to put in that hard work even when your lot is rocky and overgrown.

Commitment is a must-have because growth is often times uncomfortable.

"Do something every day that you do not want to do," said Mark Twain. As we change, we need to try and avoid making the growing pains personal. We all face discomfort, but it helps to recall that all those who have succeeded — in meeting or surpassing their own expectations — have met with similar misgivings and discomfort. Parents often attempt to shelter their children from negative experiences. Although they do so out of love and concern, it is good to remember what Abraham Lincoln said: "The worst thing you can do for those you love is to do the things they could and should do for themselves." If we take away the growing experience from another, we have not helped that person in the end. We have not allowed him or her to fail and to learn. By not allowing others to make mistakes, we prevent them from growing, since growth is a slow process involving decision-making and application. In this sense, you are your own child. It may bother you to see yourself go through the changes and all the discomfort that goes with them, but wouldn't it bother you more not to grow to meet your dreams?

Finding Balance

As you become more accustomed to conscious goal-setting and implementation, take some time to think about your life and how balanced it is. Are you very focused in some areas while ignoring others? For instance, it won't matter how wealthy you are if you ignore your health. It won't matter how professionally valuable you are if you have ignored your family to make it happen. Take a few moments to really think about the various "compartments" of your life:

- *Physical* — What kind of physical or nutritional program are you following?

- *Family* — What relationships in your family do you want to strengthen?

- *Financial* — How much money do you need to feel secure?

- *Professional* — How are you becoming more valuable?

- *Community Involvement* — What are you doing to serve others in your community?

- *Mental* — In which areas do you wish to gain more knowledge?

- *Social* — How are you making time to recharge yourself and to connect with others?

- *Spiritual* — What are you striving for spiritually?

While it is true that great goals are reached when we are "driven," often the attainment of a key milestone is a chance for you not, of course, to rest on your laurels but to take stock of areas of your life that have been neglected. Thus, we often hear of government officials leaving public life to find time to pursue a creative project, spend time with family, etc.

How Balanced Is Your Life?

Rate your current state in each of the following areas of your life, with 10 being the highest and 0 being the lowest:

1. Health and Fitness

Might include: weight, aerobic capacity, strength, frequency and degree of illness, diet, body image.

Lowest   Highest

| 0 | 1 | 2 | 3 | 4 | 5 | 6 | 7 | 8 | 9 | 10 |

2. Family and Relationships

Might include: relationships with spouse or other intimate partners, relationship with children, plans for having children, relationships with siblings, relationships with parents, relationships with other relatives.

Lowest   Highest

| 0 | 1 | 2 | 3 | 4 | 5 | 6 | 7 | 8 | 9 | 10 |

3. Financial Security

Might include: current salary, retirement savings, investments, college fund, vacation fund, emergency fund, debt management, real estate.

Lowest   Highest

| 0 | 1 | 2 | 3 | 4 | 5 | 6 | 7 | 8 | 9 | 10 |

4. Career

Might include: continuing education, job satisfaction, increased pay, management/promotion, professional licensure, membership in professional societies, awards, career change.

Lowest										Highest
0	1	2	3	4	5	6	7	8	9	10

5. Community Involvement

Might include: service organizations, volunteer work, civic committees, mentoring.

Lowest										Highest
0	1	2	3	4	5	6	7	8	9	10

6. Intellectual & Personal Growth

Might include: reading literature and non-fiction, listening to self-improvement CDs, attending self-improvement seminars or support groups, improving vocabulary and communication skills.

Lowest										Highest
0	1	2	3	4	5	6	7	8	9	10

7. Social Involvement

Might include: making new friends and acquaintances, dressing and looking your best, taking part in leisure and recreational activities, trying out new social spaces and activities.

Lowest										Highest
0	1	2	3	4	5	6	7	8	9	10

8. Spiritual Enrichment

Might include: regularly attending religious services, reading spiritual literature, learning about other religions, spending time in meditation and prayer, making an effort to be compassionate toward others.

Lowest										Highest
0	1	2	3	4	5	6	7	8	9	10

How Round Is Your Wheel?

After completing the questions in the above table, look at the score for each of the eight qualifiers. Are your scores all threes, sixes or nines? Or do your scores run the gamut from one through ten? Are your scores pretty consistent, or does one stand out as unusually high or low? Typically, when we think of a wheel or tire, the more round or even it is all around, the better. How round is your wheel? What stands out to you? What does this exercise reveal that you might not have consciously been aware of? Are there any areas you need to address? How important are these areas of your life? And how do they interrelate? How do all of them feed, directly or indirectly, your Major Definite Purpose?

The rounder your wheel and the clearer your goals, the closer you will be to arriving at your destination. To use another metaphor, the human mind is like a parachute; it functions best when it is open. We need to focus on the overall goal but be open to possibilities. Psychologist Bobbe Summer says, "Hang on tight, with an open palm."

As you are reading this book, radio, television and phone signals are going through the same room that you are in. If you don't own or don't turn on the device that uses those signals, the fact that they are there is of no consequence.

You will find that, as you become more focused, you tend to ask the right questions and meet the people who can help you. The more you work on yourself and work toward your clear goals, the more success you will find.

Everything we need to be successful is accessible to us right now; we just may not be aware of it.

Goal-Setting Checklist

_____ 1. Decide what you want.

_____ 2. Develop a personal sense of purpose.

_____ 3. Get committed.

_____ 4. Consider the potential benefits/consequences.

_____ 5. Write down your long-term and short-term plans.

_____ 6. Keep your plan focused on what *you* want and

        what *you* can control.

_____ 7. Get as specific as possible.

_____ 8. Set a reasonable timeframe.

_____ 9. Keep a record.

_____ 10. Commit to ongoing improvement.

Chapter
9

Leader of the Pack

*"You have achieved excellence as a leader when people will follow
you everywhere if only out of curiosity."*
- Colin Powell

Imagine a Want-Ad that reads: "Looking for a person who is honest, committed, teaches by example, and is able to solve problems; must possess self-knowledge, an understanding of human nature, and a sense of personal responsibility; must provide purpose, direction, and motivation for self and others." Would you respond to such an ad? Many people who fit this description shy away from seeing themselves as leaders.

But the truth is, we are all in the business of leadership. We lead at work, at school, and in our family lives. We are constantly trying to persuade others to adopt our point of view. We are always negotiating with others or, at times even, with ourselves. We are always trying to influence other's decision-making. There are numerous techniques to accomplish this, some more positive than others. The key is to find out what will work for the person you are trying to influence.

Several years ago, the American Management Association conducted in-depth interviews with 41 executives and uncovered seven common traits that frequently cause leaders to fail. They include:

♦ Insensitivity to co-workers.

♦ Aloofness and arrogance.

♦ Tendency to misuse information conveyed in confidence.

♦ Inability to control ambition.

♦ Inability to delegate assignments.

♦ Inability to promote teamwork.

♦ Inability to staff effectively.

♦ Inability to think strategically.

How can leaders maintain the difficult balance of managing the affairs of the company, family or team while maintaining their loyalty? What truly sets apart a mediocre, overbearing boss from a highly respected and effective leader?

The answer is that effective leaders inspire others to perform better than they thought possible. Top notch leaders also lead their families, their friends, as well as the people with whom they work. A leader is someone whom others consistently follow. Thus it stands to reason that people follow because they have a belief in the direction, integrity and competence of the one leading. Surveys consistently indicate that people seek honest, forward-looking, inspiring and competent persons in positions of leadership.

Characteristics of Leadership

Confidence	Openness to risk
Discipline	Honesty
Enthusiasm	Adaptability
Creativity	Team orientation
Knowledge	Fairness
Loyalty	Decisiveness
Ability to listen	Planning skills
Ability to motivate	Perceptiveness

Why Should They Follow?"

When trying to influence another individual, the question that has to be answered is, "What's in it for them?"   Until you can answer that question effectively, it may be difficult to get others to "buy in" to what you have in mind. People are generally motivated by either emotional or material incentives:

Emotional Benefits	Material Benefits
Recognition	Money
Achievement	Time
Security	Efficiency
Pleasure	Improvement
Self-Confidence	Safety

When trying to motivate others, it's best to have a clear sense of how their cooperation will benefit them either emotionally or materially — or, preferably, on both levels if possible. The more potential benefits we can provide, the more likely they will be supportive and willing to embrace suggestions.

> *As a friend of mine says about church attendance, "If you can't get the flock to attend every week, it doesn't matter how right you are."*

Many of us try to lead in a way that is most conducive for us, which typically translates to the easiest way. By "easiest," I mean that we lead based on factors such as convenience, time or our own psychological make-up. We typically apply techniques we've seen others employ, or we try to lead in the way we would like to be led. In consulting with companies, I have often seen managers or foremen struggle in leadership roles. They may or may not admit that the leadership role is difficult for them, but others pick up on it. In most cases, they were very good at their jobs and were promoted with little or no leadership/management training. The rationale being that they already know how to do the job, so why would they need additional training? But the truth of the matter is that knowing how to perform the technical side of the position does not mean that an individual is qualified to function in a leadership capacity.

Many ineffective leaders simply use techniques they've seen others use; more often, they base their leadership style on how they would want to be led. This may work but only if others share the philosophy and style. Unfortunately many of the problems that can develop for leaders have to do with their ability to relate to others.

We believe and act similarly to those whom we value and trust. As far as beliefs and values are concerned, people generally follow others' examples. As an example, athletes who go on to coach typically coach in the manner they were coached, adopting the philosophy that their coaches displayed. Yet, when pressed to explain why they coach and believe what they do, they may have a hard time putting it into words. They know that other philosophies have been successfully used by other coaches with different styles; they just unconsciously disregard them because they are not familiar with them.

On the other hand, when we see some flaw in the philosophy or behavior of leaders to whom we're exposed, a leader's negative style can be a catalyst that inspires us to adopt different values, beliefs and approaches - in hopes of changing now what we couldn't change in our past. Either way, we are influenced by those we deemed important, and they help formulate our value and belief systems. While influences are important, you will strengthen your leadership capacity by looking at ways in which you - given your personality and values - can best get others to share your vision.

What Leaders Must Do

Effective leadership cannot be reduced to simple cookbook recipes. However, there are general principles, attributes and skills which apply to most situations. If practiced systematically, these techniques will address most issues and, at the same time will allow the leader to be well-positioned to handle the problems that do require individualized solutions. Before specific techniques can be effective, though, certain key attitudes must be present. Since these attitudes and behaviors complement one another to form a systematic approach, attempts to use parts of the system as isolated techniques or gimmicks generally do not work in the long term.

First, **leaders must respect others as individuals**. They don't need to be overly dramatic, but they must show concern for other individuals. This is shown through tone of voice, facial expressions and other non-verbal behavior. A leader who is standoffish can be perceived as "cold" and may seem to be talking *at* rather than *to* others, despite good intentions.

Second, **leaders must establish and maintain credibility.** Most of us have been exposed to inconsistencies between what leaders preach and what they practice. We may even automatically assume, when we see such inconsistencies, that the leader is trying to "con" us, seeing genuine expressions of concern as attempts to manipulate us for ulterior motives. Credibility is established largely by making sure that words and actions coincide. Credibility provides structure. If people can depend on what leaders say, they will be less likely to be tested constantly. A leader's accountability helps others to accept responsibility for their own behavior. Since appropriate expectations are also involved in establishing credibility, leaders must think through what they really expect from others and then ensure that their own behavior is consistent with those expectations. This is also called leading by example which, in and of itself, builds credibility.

Third, **there is no reason for leaders to do what others can do for themselves**. Leaders often say, "I tried to get them to do it for themselves, but they couldn't." But this focuses on the short-term solution instead of looking at the bigger picture. It also communicates low expectations for others, reinforcing their limitations or unwillingness to stretch their abilities. Alternatively, when people understand why they are expected to do something and are given the correct tools and training to do it, they generally perform to expectations.

Problems, Issues and Troubleshooting

As a leader, you will constantly be faced with challenges. The more quickly and easily we learn to address these challenges, the less stressed we will be, and the more effective we will be viewed as leaders. As with other parts of this book, a systematic approach may help you with the problem-solving process. Here is a four-step approach to problems that is as useful in professional leadership as it is in personal leadership situations.

Define the problem. This requires good communication. Make sure from the outset that you have a clear understanding of what the problem is. It is amazing how much time can be wasted on false assumptions or in trying to get a firm grasp on what the "real" problem is.

What are the possible causes? Look for the obvious and the not-so-obvious causes of the problem. What assumptions were made that led to the problem? Just as you would not want your physician to make assumptions about your medical condition, don't assume that you know what has caused the problem without a thorough investigation.

Ask others for their ideas/solutions. Ask others involved in or effected by the problem what they think should be done. Avoid the tendency to take on all problems as your own. Sometimes, the best solution is to do nothing at all. While other times, the best solution is to gather additional information. Be conscious of the fact that all problems have more than one solution and do not all have to be handled by you, as the leader.

Create responsibility for finding and implementing a solution. Once you have decided on a number of possible solutions, set a deadline for arriving at one solution. Then create a timetable for its implementation. Try to make it a habit to follow these steps — for all types of problems. With practice, solving problems will become a part of the process and not a major disruption.

Personal Acceptance and Independence. Understanding who you are and what your needs are will help you to identify your best leadership style — as will understanding your need for personal acceptance. Our need for acceptance is connected to our self-concept. When our ideas are accepted or rejected, do we take the issue personally or do we separate the decision from our sense of personal worth? Acceptance is also linked to our need for inclusion. Some individuals need to be included and involved with a group; others work by themselves. An extreme need for acceptance can even cause some leaders to avoid taking action for fear of criticism and rejection. In short, to what degree does your need for acceptance effect your decision-making, and how it is projected in your leadership style. It's important to understand how strong your need for acceptance is.

Your need for acceptance is	
High if ...	**Low if ...**
You set easy goals for yourself	You constantly challenge yourself
Your self-confidence comes from others	Your self-confidence comes from within
You tend to procrastinate	You tend to take action
You have difficulty not taking criticism	You can be objective about personal criticism

The counter to acceptance is independence. For our purposes here, we are discussing independence in two ways, personal independence and the independence you project as a leader.

- How independent are you?
- Do you need validation from others or are you comfortable with who you are?
- Do you need to be popular?
- Are you comfortable giving others the opportunity to work alone?

The manner in which you answer these questions reflects your leadership style.

Your need for independence is	
High if ...	**Low if ...**
You resist the advice of others	You consult with others before decisions
You are mostly self-reliant	You rely on others a great deal
You are comfortable alone	You need to be with others
You need a deadline	You need a deadline

Fear Works, but Only in the Short Term

Leaders must understand motivation in order to effectively motivate others. If a leader is getting results without this understanding, it is potentially just luck. In the long run, understanding drives motivation.

> *The more reasons we have to do something and the stronger those reasons, the more motivated and determined we become.*

Among the different ways of motivating yourself and others to do or not do something, the most common is through fear. Fear motivation works with some people, some of the time. The downside to this form of motivation is that it typically is only temporarily effective, and ever-increasing doses are needed for it to continue being effective. Some professional coaches use these techniques with young teams and typically get results fairly quickly. They are also coaches who tend to change teams rather frequently as, after a while, players become desensitized to this approach, and the coach is no longer effective.

Supply Enough Carrots and Any Horse Will Go Forward

The second type of motivation is incentive-driven. We have all heard of the proverbial carrot in front of the horse. For this to work, the horse has to be hungry and the load light enough to pull. This type of motivation is most commonly employed to get people to move forward, too. There does come a time, however, when a given "carrot" no longer works, and different and increasing amounts of motivation are needed. If getting our children to do their chores is linked to their weekly allowance, there may come a time when they would rather not do their chores because the allowance is not large enough. If this is our only motivational tactic, we become stuck. The same is true for adults. In business, if money is the sole way in which employees are motivated, there may come a time when we can't match their pay demands. Once an incentive is obtained, in any area of life, there's often a sense of "What more?" or "What next?" Good leaders find other ways to fill that void for themselves and those around them.

Encourage People to Grow

The third, more meaningful, motivator is that of change or growth. The purpose here is to lead in a way that models openness to change and growth, encouraging those around you to embrace it as well. If we can get others to "buy in" to our goals in this way, we are truly leading from the front. We are providing the tools necessary for others to succeed.

Leaders should understand and respond to the needs of others. To understand, we have to listen. If we aren't truly listening, then we will base our acts on assumptions, and those assumptions may or may not be correct. This is why the cookie-cutter approach to dealing with people doesn't work. People perceive information differently. Everyone is different and has different likes/dislikes, motivators and "hot buttons." Only through listening can we understand others well enough to work with them.

I was once surprised to hear a dock foreman at a company I consulted for tell me that he was not interested in getting to know his people. What was the sense, he reasoned, since they all quit shortly after they had been there for a couple of months. Besides, he added, it wasn't his job to relate to them in any way other than to tell them how to do their job. He made it clear that he didn't want to know anything about their personal lives and that he was not a babysitter. Is it any wonder they quit? It's no wonder that after hearing this three years ago, the company is now considering filing for bankruptcy. I am certainly not saying that the failure of this company was solely the result of this dock foreman. But think of it this way: What type of person would you want to be led by - someone who supports you or someone who shows indifference? If you would want to be supported, support others.

"It is only as we develop others that we permanently succeed." - Harvey Firestone

Help Others to Help Themselves

"Being a leader is like being a lady. If you have to tell people you are, you aren't," Margaret Thatcher has wittily observed. People buy into the person before they buy into that person's leadership. If we can make the personal contact work, the rest becomes much easier. Remember, we don't want to portray ourselves as better than anyone else. What is the point? If we are better, let our actions speak for themselves. If we aren't better but act like it, people will resent us and will not be willing to support us. Leaders must constantly show that they care. It goes without saying your answers to the following questions will closely relate to how others view you as an actual or potential leader.

- ♦ How important do others feel when they are around you?
- ♦ When was the last time you made it possible for others to be proud of their accomplishments?
- ♦ What have you done to show others how important they are?
- ♦ How often do you celebrate others' successes?

As a leader, look to influence, inspire and inform. If we can succeed in these three areas, we will be successful. Great leaders don't try to get people to believe in them; rather, they show people how to believe in themselves. Anyone can be told what to do. A leader helps others find their own way to the same destination. A leader needs to be more concerned with helping others achieve what they want (empowerment) and less concerned with helping themselves (power).   Scott Klein says, "Leadership is the ability to teach people and organizations to surpass themselves."

Four Action Steps for Leaders Who Empower Others

Provide regular, measurable and observable feedback related to performance. In business, this might mean making time - at regular and reasonable intervals - for written or in-person recognition of ways in which team members or staff have handled day-to-day as well as unusual challenges. On a more personal level, it might mean taking time to thank friends for helping you through a particularly challenging time.

Be accessible. In today's business world, being accessible is key. Technology has made this simpler, and it is expected. On a personal level, email and cell phones may have made the written letter a thing of the past, but communication is still just as practical as ever.

Provide support for others' ideas.   Allow others to be creative. Many of our most ingenious ideas have come from "what if's" supported by time to work on these projects. In our personal lives, creativity has also led the way to many positive breakthroughs.

Make quick decisions. As a leader, the ability to make quick decisions is key.   Today's business world is changing quickly. Many companies have vanished simply because of their inability to make decisions.   The same is true personally. Good opportunities do not always linger. The quicker we can identify them and take action, the quicker we will move forward.

See the Future; Create the Vision

Leaders need to have long-term awareness. They need not only to see the present situation but also to relate to the past while projecting to the future. Having a long-term plan does not mean that success is a certainty. It does, however, mean that we have taken time to consider the future and what the best- and worst-case scenarios may be. This is because good leaders respond rather than react, and projecting and planning allow for quicker responses. They aren't taken off-guard when something goes wrong, because they have already thought about it. The more long-term planning you do, the more proactive you will be.

Success, it is said, is the result of good judgment. Good judgment is the result of experience, and bad experiences are often the result of bad judgment.

Another way of looking at long-term planning is to consider our vision. What is our vision, be it for yourself or your company? Have you created a vision, or are you too busy to plan? Do you want things to just happen or do you want to be in control? Create a vision. The second question becomes: Are you behaving in ways that are likely to make that vision a reality? I do believe that we all should have a personal vision and also a vision related to our careers, relationships, finances, spiritual life, etc. In this sense, we are all leaders, even if only of our own lives. Are you sharing your vision with others? If you aren't sharing, how clear is it to others? If you aren't sharing, is it possible that others may be misinterpreting your actions? Decide, what you want to make happen. Decide with the best information you have at the time, what course of action you intend to follow. Listen to others tell their stories. Tell others of your desire to get their input and to put yourself on the line.

> *"Nothing can resist a will which will stake even existence upon its fulfillment."*
> - Beniamin Disraeli

You should be able to create a concise statement related to your vision. If you cannot describe it, how can others follow it? **A vision can't be forced on others.** You can, however, describe it, refer to it, and act like it is important to you.

Leadership is getting others to compromise for the good of all, and a future vision is important for getting others to make such compromises when times get tough. When Christopher Columbus was searching for the New World, his crew became discouraged and demanded that he turn back. Columbus compromised with them, promising that, if they would be patient and faithful just three days longer, he would abandon the enterprise, unless land was discovered. Within three days, land appeared, and the rest is history.

Not only do leaders inspire others to compromise for the sake of the future, but, at times, they need to make sacrifices in order to show others how important their visions are. An excellent example of this was Alexander the Great who, in the fourth century, b.c., led his troops across a hot and desolate plain. After a number of days, he and all his soldiers were nearly dead from thirst. Alexander pressed on. One day, at noon, two scouts brought him what little water they had found, which barely filled a cup. Alexander's troops stood and watched as he poured the water into the hot sand, proclaiming, "It is no use for one to drink when many thirst." Being a leader, Alexander gave his followers the only thing he had at the time - inspiration. That inspiration rested on the foundation of his vision.

Bringing Others into Your Vision

In the business world, much is said about the importance of getting people to "buy in" to a vision, mission or project. It's another way of saying that it is important, in business and elsewhere, to develop relationships with people who will invest in your vision. How do you create a "buy in" mentality? I believe that one important way is to work or associate with people who are capable and likely to want to buy in.

You don't want to reinvent the wheel; you want to start out with a wheel and make it better.

If you spend too much time trying to convert those who are not interested, you are taking time away from those who do want to be involved. If you are an employer, this means hiring people with good attitudes.   Kevin and Jackie Freiberg, authors of the book, *Nuts*, have a saying they use in their consulting work: "Hire people that don't suck . . . the life out of your company." The same could be said for our personal relationships and the importance of associating with people who believe the way you do or share a baseline of common beliefs. Unless you're a missionary, you're not trying to convert people. You are trying to help them and help yourself.

"Buy in" is created through delegating. Delegating allows everyone to have a degree of ownership in the decision-making process and the steps along the way to your goal. If we're acting as good leaders, when the task is accomplished, the others will say that they did it themselves. Always let them know that, if their action leads to success, the accolades will be theirs and, if there is failure, you will take the blame. If we teach responsibility and accountability, then delegate decision-making and authority, we will have an easier time interacting with others and getting them to do what we want. Why? Because doing what we want will also get them to where they want to be.

Look to associate with others who are smarter than we are in key areas. In this way, we learn from them and become stronger. No one person - not even a genius - is so well-rounded that he or she knows it all. In some ways, you have a leg up on even Einstein. Feels better that way, doesn't it? We can't do it all by ourselves. It all goes back to the concept of leverage. Through leverage of resources - people, time, and money - we can get to where we want to be, assuming that we know where we want to be and are not taking advantage of others to get there.

If we help others get what they want, they will help us get where we want.

J. C. Penney knew that, if he empowered his employees, they would make him rich.

How do we influence others so that they invest in our vision? One way is through reciprocation. If we do something for someone, that person will be more likely to want to do something for us. That makes sense. We have all heard of one hand washing the other. It's easiest to get someone to do something for us when there is a perception that we have already done something for them. This perception can be real or imagined, but, if it is there, it helps in influencing reciprocal behavior.

Influencing others to invest in what you're doing is by being consistent. We like to work or be with people who do what they say they will do. They don't keep us guessing, and we don't have to constantly check up on them to see that they are doing what they said they would. The connection here is that leaders teach responsibility and therefore have higher expectations for others, expectations that are likely to be met if they themselves are consistent.

People are naturally drawn to people like themselves. Salespeople have been keyed in to this for years, and it's good to keep in mind when you hope to influence others. If we appear to be like those we want to influence, neither above nor below their perceptions, we will have an easier time influencing their decision-making.

Another way to influence others to invest in your vision is to offer positive approaches to negative events or situations. Military history will bear this out from thousands or years of conflict. Outside conflict is always a unifying force. The wagons get circled in times of peril. People are apt to be lead because they are unsure of what action to take individually and thus go with the "herd" mentality following the crowd that is following the strongest leader.

Follow the Leader

Leaders build a following. If a leader doesn't build a following, he or she may be the leader in name but won't have the power of influence, and, without influence, power is ineffective and temporary.

Leaders put others in positions that allow them to succeed.

"The best executive is the one who has the sense enough to pick good men to do what he wants done, and self-restraint enough to keep from meddling with them while they do it," Theodore Roosevelt said.   If someone is failing, it may be because he or she doesn't have the skills or has been put into the wrong position.

Leaders build followings when they constantly look for opportunity, especially in adversity.   It's in these times that we learn the most.   Whether one is a parent, a teacher or a public official, leaders are always being observed and, frequently, model action for others.   People look to those in leadership roles to see how they handle themselves and their situations day in and day out.   Leaders are under even more acute observation during a crisis, for this is when our leadership qualities are most needed and when they are more apt to be challenged.

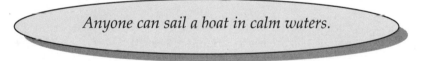

Anyone can sail a boat in calm waters.

Leaders are also under scrutiny after a crisis.   What is the fallout from the unexpected crisis?   What created the problem, and how can it be handled so that it does not happen again?   If you think of yourself as always being on camera, you are more apt to understand that others (employees, friends, family) as always watching.   They are not necessarily being critical; they are, however, constantly collecting information that supports or detracts from their opinion of you.   What they see influences their willingness to share your vision and join forces with you.

Secrets to Leadership

1. Use self-deprecating humor, which helps others to see you as more human.

2. Be careful of others' feelings. What is funny to you may not be to others.

3. Make other people feel important. The better they feel, the more they will do for you.

4. Make your cause bigger than you, since common goals equal greater success.

4. Recognize your own strengths, but don't let them hinder others.

5. Recognize your own weaknesses. We all have them.

6. Be solution-oriented, not problem-oriented, looking not only at what doesn't work but also at what does work.

7. Your actions speak louder than your words, so act as though you are always being observed.

8. As much as possible, act unselfishly. Leadership is a team sport — not an individual one.

Find What You Are Looking for

Observing is a two-sided process. If you want to connect well with others, look for the good in them. Catch them doing their best, and recognize them for it. Seize the opportunity to praise their actions and decision-making. This is the surest way to empower them to continue to try their best. Just as positive thinking and self-image help you individually to meet your own purpose and goals, they help you to lead others to strive for more. Whether you are in a leadership role now or are merely thinking about what your leadership potential might be, the logical "next step" after getting to know yourself and what you want is to consider how you can best work with others to reach goals that are important to you. Here are some concepts that are worth keeping in mind as you refine your interpersonal skills:

- **Relationship** – How well do I know people?

- **Attitude** – Do I tend to look for the good in others?

- **Communication** – How well can I motivate people through my words and example?

- **Leadership** – What is my influential style, and is it the best for every situation I face?

Your answers to these questions will provide a starting point from which you can honestly put yourself on the line and expect the best from yourself and others. "People don't care how much you know, until they know how much you care." Zig Ziglar has said. Caring leaders document and praise accomplishments in public, using success to reinforce others' confidence. When they do criticize, it is in private and is connected with the performance and not the person.

Leaders view failure as a not-to-be-repeated learning experience.

Leaders encourage experimentation and tolerate mistakes. Leaders are constantly improving themselves and expecting more of others. Maybe you already view yourself as a leader; maybe you're considering whether you're leadership material. If you've begun to take real charge of your own life, you've already begun to be a leader. And, the better handle you have on who you are and what you want, the more likely you'll serve as a beacon to others with whom you come into contact. Thus, we're all potential leaders, even if we don't carry a title.

Questions for Self-Assessment

1. What motivates you most to do something difficult?

2. How do you show others that you care?

3. Do you have a long-term vision that others know about?

4. Have you been able to get people around you to "buy in" to your vision?

5. What is something you can do for someone whom you hope to influence?

6. Can you think of a problem you face that might actually be an opportunity?

7. How high are your expectations for yourself? For others?

8. When was the last time you praised someone?

Change is Inevitable; Growth is Optional

"Get busy living or get busy dying."
—Stephen King, The Shawshank Redemption

If we want to have a more positive life experience, we must be convinced that any change we make will fulfill a particular need or desire. Positive self-motivation begins with changing our awareness. To make constructive changes in our lives, we must evaluate the potential benefits for any given action. Then we must convince ourselves that the benefits will justify or outweigh the price we have to pay for them. Others may inspire or threaten us to make a change, but it's up to us to motivate ourselves. This often happens once we do a benefits vs. cost comparison and find that the benefits far outweigh the costs. To some degree, we have been doing this all our lives, only now, we can become more conscious about the process and therefore make it more likely to work for us.

"If you're not the lead dog,
the scenery never changes."
- Ken Blanchard

In contemplating whether or not to make a big change, start by being as objective as possible with yourself, even though true objectivity is practically impossible. Many of our decisions are based upon our sense of the truth when, in reality, that "truth" has come from other subjective individuals, as well from biased media and entertainment sources. If we question ourselves and think long enough, we can create doubt even in our own minds. This is because it's often easier to accept assumptions without determining if they are factually grounded or even considering whether or not we really believe that they are true. Studies have found, for example, that people tend to ask actors who play doctors on television shows for medical advice. Does this logically make sense? The answer is "no", but that doesn't change the phenomenon, a phenomenon which shows the extent to which much of our beliefs are borrowed from media images rather than based on objective realities.

"When dealing with people, let us remember we are not dealing with creatures of logic. We are dealing with creatures of emotion." - Dale Carnegie

It just makes sense to become aware of your beliefs and ideas when contemplating change or when dealing with the changes that life inevitably brings.

> *Change can happen instantaneously,*
> *but it will not occur without a trigger.*

In order for change to occur, there must be a catalyst. I recently watched the demolition of Veterans Stadium in Philadelphia. The actual detonation that brought down the entire stadium took less than one minute. In fact, they claimed that the demolition was actually slower than usual due to the close proximity of housing. What took the most time was the preparation of the site for the demolition: explosives had to be placed, certain steel beams cut, permits needed to be secured, extra police had to be brought in, and neighbors had to be evacuated. This is generally how big life changes take place. When we are ready, the actual change is quick. It is the getting ready to change that takes all the time and effort.

Individuals don't change without a reason or motive. Even if they decide to go against their typical patterned behaviors, there is a usually a compelling reason for their new behavior. Typically, there must be a problem before a change can occur. That makes sense, doesn't it? Why change if everything is working perfectly, and no threat is on the horizon? To change, we need to desire a new or different outcome. The main thing to remember is that, when you find yourself feeling that a change is necessary, that nagging need for change is a message you should try to hear. If not you, then who? If not now, then when?

> *For change to be beneficial there must be a compelling "why."*

We need to realize that the way things are is not the way we want them to be. We have to decide to stop accepting the norm as our best. We have decided to break out of our own comfort levels and to strive for more. Whether we desire change in our personal relationships, our body shape and weight, our financial status, or our business ventures, the concepts for change are the same. We have to establish why we need to change. This helps in defining our current status and also helps to deepen our desire. When we know precisely what we want, we become more alert to what can help us. Without a strong "why," it's too easy to be indecisive and to procrastinate. And so, when we're looking forward to any substantial change, the "why" must come first.

The Mind Matters

The greatest psychological barriers we face are self-imposed. In one of Houdini's most famous and spectacular feats, escaping from Scotland Yard, one of the conditions of the challenge was that he be placed in the cell naked, in order to keep him from concealing tools or keys. So how did he do it? Quite simply, using a razor blade, he cut a small, invisible slit in a heavy callus on his heel. Under this tiny flap of hardened skin, he concealed a small piece of watch spring. Then, once he was alone, he used this little strip of metal to pick all the locks, then tossed the tool way and walked out!

Looking to capitalize on Houdini's immense popularity and fame, a London bank challenged him to break out of their vault with its new, state-of-the-art locking system. They were certain that even the great Houdini would finally meet his match. Houdini accepted, and, on the appointed date, the press turned out to see if the master could get out in the three and a half minutes allotted.

This time, he was allowed to keep his clothes on. But he had another trick up his sleeve. His contract always specified that, before he disappeared into the trunk or cell or behind a small curtain, he could kiss his wife. After all, many of his feats were dangerous, so who could refuse the couple what might turn out to be their final goodbye? What no one knew was that he was getting more than a kiss. As their lips met, his wife would secretly pass a small piece of wire from her mouth to his. Then, once he was alone and hidden behind the curtain, he'd use the wire to pick the locks.

This time, though, the wire didn't seem to be doing the trick. Here's what Houdini wrote about that experience: "After one solid minute, I didn't hear any of the familiar clicking sounds. I thought, this could ruin my career, I'm at the pinnacle of fame, and the press is all here. After two minutes, I was beginning to sweat profusely because I was not getting this lock picked. After three minutes of failure, with thirty seconds left, I reached into my pocket to get a handkerchief and dry my hands and forehead, and when I did, I leaned against the vault door and it creaked open."

There you have it.   The door was never locked!   But because Harry believed it to be locked, it might as well have been.   Only the "accident" of leaning on the door changed that belief and saved his career.   It's the same way with all of us.   The things we believe to be insurmountable barriers, obstacles and problems are just like the bank vault door.

> *The only lock is in our minds, and as long as we simply believe we can't, we can't.*

Does this sound familiar?   Some people go through life as if they were dragging a large anchor behind them weighing them down.   If they could release it, they would be able to move more quickly and succeed more easily.   If you have ever tried to drive a car with the emergency brake on, you know what I'm talking about.   Something just doesn't "feel right."   Releasing these anchors or brakes can allow us to more easily move toward being the successful people we are capable of being.

Let's look at another example of the same limiting principle.   Humans have learned how to train elephants using their own minds against them.   When baby elephants are very young, weighing about 150 pounds, they are shackled with a heavy rope or chain.   At first, the elephants struggle with all of their energy, but, because they are so small, they can't break their bonds.   Over time, they realize that struggling doesn't work and resign themselves to the fact that they are imprisoned by the spike. In fact, their bonds become purely mental. From that moment, they strongly believe that there is no chance to get rid of their bonds. They accept the fact that their bonds limit them. As the elephant grows, the same chain and spike are used. Even as adults, weighing eight thousand pounds and more, the elephants don't attempt to break free because they "know" they have no chance. The elephants grow and become easily capable of freeing themselves, only they don't try. They are imprisoned by an almost imaginary cage.

Let the example of the elephant serve as an example not of being shackled but of what we are capable of when we get beyond mental barriers. We are all programmed with built-in boundaries. But with these imprinted belief systems, with these inner boundaries, we are unable . . .

- ♦ To live our lives to the fullest.
- ♦ To be successful as we could be.
- ♦ To set and reach higher goals.
- ♦ To make more money than we do now.
- ♦ To have better relationships than we do now.
- ♦ To build a successful business.
- ♦ To get that promotion we want.
- ♦ To fulfill our true dreams and desires.

If we truly want to become successful and are not kidding ourselves, we can change our inner belief system, our attitudes and our inner boundaries. We always have the inner strength, the personal power to change everything in our lives for the better.

Question Everything

Don't be like the elephant - question what is holding you back. The right questions lead to quality answers. If we aren't satisfied with our current situation, we need to ask ourselves insightful questions that will lead to quality answers. Our questions will lead us to our path. Have you seen the television commercial with the tag line: "Question everything"? In many ways, that statement is very true. The more focused our questions, the more focused our answers will be. If our ideas are muddled and unclear, our self-talk will be lost in ambiguities.

We must know what the problem is, and we must be committed to changing it.

Asking ourselves enough of the right questions allow us to deal more easily with our subjective selves and escape illogical fears. As we keep asking questions, the answers become clearer.

Questions also allow us to get away from quick preconceived answers. Children often ask "Why?" again and again. As adults, we struggle to provide different answers to the same question. Since children look for an answer that they can understand, not one we can understand, we must answer their question on their level. The same is true with us as adults.

We must continue to try and find deeper meanings within ourselves.

If an answer to your question keeps you, like a child, asking "Why?", then, just as you would do with a child, keep searching for the answer that rings true. Here are some questions to ask to get a sense of whether or not you're comfortable with the way things are:

- Are you the type of leader/parent/athlete, etc. you want to be?
- Are you energized, doing what you want to do?
- Are you doing your best work?
- Are you in the right situation to build the future you want to build?

I know a woman who smoked for approximately fifty years of her life. Her son developed cancer, and, although not proven, it was attributed to second-hand smoke. Her son grew up in a house where he did not smoke, but both parents did. His mother, who received pleasure from smoking, suddenly was in massive pain. The new realization that she may have contributed to her son getting cancer caused her to stop smoking immediately, and she has not smoked since. Her condition did not change, but her association of smoking with pleasure did.

Being aware of the pain/pleasure principle allows us to ask better questions, to develop better understanding, and to make the cost-benefit analysis necessary for conscious change. Be aware that, usually, we will do more to avoid pain than to seek pleasure. Most of us will work harder to not be punished than we will to get ahead. Most will work harder to protect what we have than to attain something new. But you can use this fact of human nature to push yourself in the direction in which you should go. In problem solving, decide what the worst- and best-case scenario is and then work backward. If we can picture the best and worst, we can use that as a motivator to change. Decide where you are.

Decide what behaviors have gotten you there. Decide what will happen if you don't change. Next, associate pain with not taking action. Decide what will happen if you do take action, being very conscious of the pleasurable rewards of change. Use either or both of these forces to assist you in your change.

Change Right Now

♦ What action have you been putting off?
♦ Why haven't you taken action?
♦ What pleasure are you receiving from this action?
♦ What pain will you receive if you don't change?
♦ Why do you want to change?
♦ What pleasure will your new action bring you?

You Gotta Believe

To create a change, **we must believe something *must* change**, not that it should. There is a difference. When something must change, there is a stronger commitment. Knowing that it should is like a wish. Next, **address the pain/pleasure principle.** Acknowledge within yourself what you are getting from your current behavior. Third, **while acknowledging that a change must occur, we must**

believe that we are the ones who can change it. No one can really change us, and we really can't change someone else. No one can change us without our permission. In the end, we are the source of our own thoughts, and thus we alone have the power to change ourselves.

What is your internal response to external events? How you answer that question ultimately defines who you are.

William Glasser's "Choice Theory" claims that, in most instances, we choose everything we do including the way we feel. And Reverend Billy Graham echoes this when he says that "I believe the only life I have changed is mine. But I keep trying to be a positive influence for others because I believe in what I say and I believe in what I am doing,"

In his book, *The Psychology of Winning*, Denis Waitley discusses perceptions: "It makes little difference what is actually happening; it's how you personally take it that really counts!"

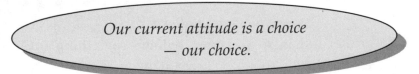

Our current attitude is a choice — our choice.

We can't control what happens to us, but we can control how we manage it. We control what associations we are linking to it. Other people cannot make us feel. It's only when we take ownership that we can feel either good or bad. Don't let what we can't do interfere with what we can do. Choose to live proactively rather than reactively. Deal with crises, and they will end in a positive way. If you look for the opportunity, not the problem, you will find what you are looking for.

> *If we are expecting a different result than what we're used to, we must try a different approach.*

To find what we can't find we must look where we haven't looked. After all, the approximate definition of insanity is performing the same action repeatedly and expecting a different result. A key difference between successful and unsuccessful people is that successful people do the things unsuccessful people don't like to do. The interesting piece to that is that successful people don't like to do them either, but they are disciplined enough to push past their reluctance. There is always a way. Keep trying until you get your desired result.

Our beliefs are shown through our words and actions. If you are committed to change, make your language consistent with your new belief. Make your actions show your new thoughts. In purposely embracing this process, self-limiting beliefs are, overtime replaced with new self-enhancing beliefs.

Moving beyond your limiting beliefs is a critical step toward becoming successful. Decide what self-limiting beliefs are holding you back.

- Are you too slow?
- Are you not smart enough?
- Do you not have enough time?

These self-limiting beliefs are excuses only in our own minds.

Make a decision today to challenge and reject those beliefs. Determine how these particular beliefs are effecting or limiting you. Decide how you want to feel or act instead. Take action (mental or physical) toward your new beliefs. Keep track of your progress and the new way you feel about yourself.

Formula for Change
- Create doubt that things can't change by asking yourself better questions.
- Believe that something *must* change, not just that it should.
- Acknowledge where you are getting your reward, pain or pleasure from the status quo.
- Get leverage — associate pain with not changing.
- Get leverage — associate pleasure with your new choices.
- Believe that you are the sole source of your change.
- Insist that you can find a way.

Choices, Choices

All of life is a series of choices, and the decisions made each day effect your tomorrow. Small changes maintained consistently can lead to big results. There is a story about basketball coach Phil Jackson asking his players at the end of a season to assess their offensive and defensive performances. He then asked each player to commit to improving one aspect of their game by ten percent. As an example, he was asking a 10-point per game scorer to commit to scoring eleven points the following year. He knew that, if he set his goals too high, the players wouldn't buy in. But, because the goal was acceptable, he could get his players to connect. What is the big deal, scoring one more point per game? The key was to get all the players to commit to being ten percent better, and, that way, individual improvements would be compounded.

Motivational guru Anthony Robbins says that "making a true decision means committing to a result, and cutting off any other possibility." In some instances, it's fear - either of what is known or of what is not - that leads us to inaction. It's okay to have fears. Admit your fears, but don't let them control you. Progress is made through conquering your fears.

> "If you want to change attitudes, start with a change in behavior"
> - William Glasser

Act the part or, as some say, "fake it until you make it." Our success in life is determined by choices we make, so don't let fear be the one making your choices.

Cause & Effect

"It's not what happens; it's what you do that makes the difference," Jim Rohn has said. Take personal responsibility both for your actions as well as for what happens to you. Consider the fact that pure chance is involved some of the time, but don't let that obscure the fact that personal choice is involved most of the time. Progress occurs only through change. If there is no change, there is no growth. The best you can hope for while not changing is the status quo. You cannot move ahead, but others who are growing can. In fact, just trying to maintain the status quo could be putting you further behind. The decisions you make or don't make shape who you become. Henry Ford said, "Whether you think you can or think you can't, you are probably right."

In the book, *Seven Habits of Highly Effective People*, Steven Covey writes of keeping the end in mind, of staying focused on our objectives while anticipating obstacles. Every swing and miss provides feedback. Stay focused and learn to make decisions quickly. List your options. Choose the best solution with the information you have at the time and move on. The more quickly we make decisions, the more quickly we will change and move toward our goals. Think of yourself as a pilot navigating at night. Your decision-making will allow you to set a course. Stay committed to your decisions but flexible in your approach. Maximum results/rewards demand all of you.

As we discussed earlier in this book, you don't have to know all of the answers. This is why modeling others and having mentors speeds up the process. Find others who have struggled with the issues you now face. We will find the answers we seek if we look hard enough.

> *Cut down on your learning curve by finding others who have forged the path to where you want to go.*

As you look for role models who have gone where you want to go, also look for activities that will take you to the same place. Are there organizations or associations that have a primary connection to what you are looking for? If so, join them. If the types of people you are looking to associate with spend time at certain venues, go there as well. The more in line you can put yourself with those you are trying to emulate, the more likely it is that your desired change will occur.

See the Real You

The starting point of all change is when we change the dominant thoughts that have been limiting our awareness. It's possible to do this because we make our own world. Change can be affected through our subconscious minds and imagination. We know from experience that an outward change will come after we change from within. By changing our dominant thoughts or beliefs, we change our awareness and our reactions to people, circumstances and conditions.

Before we can change our lives to more positive experiences, we have to get the total picture of ourselves.

Once we are able to see ourselves as others see us and our present world as it is, not as we wish it was, we're ready to start building that bridge between where we are now and where we'd like to be, from who we are now to who we'd like to become.

Try and look at yourself objectively. This is more easily said than done.

> *Part of the process of changing is acknowledging that we aren't what we think we can be or would like to be.*

Everyone has a limitation of some kind. That's why everyone can work on change. If we are satisfied with ourselves in all areas, we're either not being honest or have standards that are too low. Look at yourself through the eyes of others. What two adjectives would most people use to describe you? Why? If you can't stand to be around you, how can others? How are your interactive skills with others? What types of people gravitate toward you? What types of people gravitate away from you? What type would you prefer be around? We have a tendency to become like those we surround ourselves with. Make it a conscious choice.

Fix yourself first before you expect others to change. Leo Tolstoy said, "Everyone thinks of changing the world but no one thinks of changing themselves." We need to be constantly working harder on ourselves than others expect us to. Consider why others would want to listen to you.

What is it about you that makes others want to trust, listen to and follow you? Why would others want to help you? Honest answers to these questions will help you in more accurately determining your own current self-portrait and knowing how you want to change that portrait. To help sharpen your take on yourself, here are some questions to ask yourself.

- ♦ Do you accept yourself as you are? Why or why not?
- ♦ Would you rather be someone else? If so, who? Why?
- ♦ How well do you receive compliments?
- ♦ How do you handle criticism? Do you take it personally or relate it to your actions?

Who are you, really? We have been talking in this chapter about change and how to make that happen. Most of us take credit for our successes and assign blame for our failures. Do you have to be "right", or do you instead look for win-win solutions? How does this answer reflect on your need to change? Who are you? Who would you be if . . . ? If you aren't who you would like to be, you are carrying a heavy burden. What must change for you to unleash the person you really want to be? It doesn't matter at this point how you got here or how long you have been this way; now is the time to get real with yourself and be who you need to be, for you.

Identify the Problem

Put together a list of all the obstacles that are standing in the way of your reaching your level of success. Organize the

obstacles in order of priority. What is your largest obstacle?
If you could instantly do away with one problem in your
life, which would it be and why? Once you have identified
and prioritized your list of obstacles or problems, come up
with at least twenty possible solutions. Every obstacle that is
standing between you and what you want to accomplish has
some kind of solution. The first three to five solutions will
come easy. The next five will cause you to think harder and
dig deeper. Your last ten answers will be the most difficult
of all. Many people struggle with the last ten. However
long it takes, discipline yourself to finish the process. Many
times, solution nineteen or twenty is the one that you
ultimately use.

Once you have at least twenty answers, go back over your
list and review your answers. Then select at least one
solution that you can immediately implement. In this way,
you are taking action quickly and moving toward your
success.

Small Changes, Big Results

Earlier, I mentioned that small changes over time can lead
to big results. Small errors in judgment over time can lead to
severe consequences. The easiest example of this is a
financial one. If we have a savings account that we
withdraw from without ever depositing, it will eventually be
empty. Failure to see our financial savings as dwindling
allowed us to keep making the same mistakes. Once it's
empty, it's too late. Now we have to start all over again to
build it up.

On the other hand, $2,000 invested at 8 percent a year will be worth over $16,000 in thirty years. This is the reason why investing for retirement early is so important. Indeed, small changes over time can lead to big results over time.

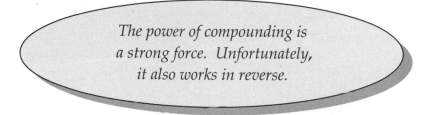

The power of compounding is a strong force. Unfortunately, it also works in reverse.

Over time, we tend to treat faulty perceptions as normal. Distortion appears more natural the longer we live with it. Think of someone who wears eyeglasses. Their eyes don't change overnight. They change gradually over time. Then one day, they go to get their eyes checked, and the optometrist tells them that their prescription glasses are no longer valid for them. They've changed. If we were to get a pair of glasses and never get our eyes checked again, we would tend to assume that those glasses were an adequate prescription for us even though they weren't.

Maybe you were not consciously planning your future. Over time, through procrastination, you may have allowed someone's plan to become your own. Admit the truth. Either ask the advice of a close friend whom you trust to tell you what you don't want to hear, or engage in your own internal dialogue. Admit there is a problem and resolve to address it. It is not how often you get off track that matters; it is how quickly you notice and what you learn that determines where you ultimately wind up.

> *A lie unchallenged becomes
> the truth over time.*

At this point, we are talking about creating a lasting change in one or many areas. Raise your standards.

> *Decide what is working and not working,
> and, in the areas that need improvement,
> demand more of yourself.*

Even you don't know for sure what you're capable of. You can make a change because others have done it, and you are as strong as or stronger than them. Continue to work at it, and change your approach until you get the result you are seeking. If you keep at it, ultimately you will find the way that works best for you. Above all, create a sense of certainty for yourself by taking control rather than looking for outside circumstances to do that. Taking control means taking responsibility, but it also means empowering yourself to change.

The Perils of Success

Enjoy but beware of your own success. The greatest enemy of tomorrow's success is today's success. I recently purchased a cookbook which included local chefs describing their best recipes. I bought the book after it had been in

Taking Control: A Pledge

♦ We control what we do with our time - how long we work, play, rest, study, worry, or procrastinate.

♦ We control how much energy we exert on any given problem or goal.

♦ We control our thoughts and attention focus.

♦ We control our attitudes.

♦ We control our communication - what we say, how we say it, and to whom.

♦ We control our personal value systems.

♦ We control our associations - whom we interact with and to what degree.

print two months; five of the restaurants described in the book were out of business. Success can lead to clouded judgment. The past doesn't equal the future. If a strategy worked once, that doesn't mean it will work the same way again. The past, in both its positive and negative aspects, is gone and won't necessarily guarantee your future.

For instance, success can lead to a more conservative approach, which may be counterproductive. Remember, we tend to do more to protect what we have than to gain more. Or success can lead to procrastination, and why not? - everything is going well. An old English proverb states, "One of these days means none of these days." The time to work on change is here and now. As the song lyric says, "These are the good old days."

Questions for Self-Assessment

1. What is changing or should change in my life that I am currently resisting?

2. Why am I resisting the change?

3. What is the benefit of not changing?

4. What are the costs of not changing?

5. What are the benefits of changing?

Chapter

11

Bringing It All Together

Just do it! - Nike

Perhaps the simplest definition of "success" is the sense of having taken charge of what you can control in your life and the sense of contentedness that comes with having done so. I have done my best to give you the principles and the tools that you will need to create your own success. These principles have worked for me and for countless others, and they can work for you as well. Nobody can do it for you! You alone are responsible for taking action and creating what you have dreamt about. But, if you stay positive and open, you'll find a lot of help and support along the way.

You have all the talent and resources you need to get started right now and to eventually create anything you want. Remember that life is a journey and that not all roads will be smooth, but all roads will lead to where you want to go if you are paying attention and know your destination.

> *You can do it; others have.*

I hope that the ideas, questions and checklists in this book will be useful to you at different points in your growth and development. As with most self-help books, some chapters more than others will speak more clearly to where you are at a given time. If a section doesn't really address your situation now, maybe, at some later point, you'll find that section helpful.

> *Our level of preparedness allows us to accept life's uncertainties.*

By way of conclusion, I'd like to leave you with some general guidelines to keep your mind focused on your own success, however you define it. These are "big picture" - type guidelines that help to put individual tasks, goals and plans in a larger perspective. The following table, for example, reviews several of the points covered in this book — with an eye to keeping your focus on what you can do *now* to take charge of where you are and where you're going, as well as to keeping your life tempo as upbeat as possible.

Let's Take Action Now

1. Decide what is working for you now. Let's keep what is working and get rid of what is holding you back.

2. Optimism and realism are connected. Take a realistic look at what you are trying to improve. Realism is the starting point, but optimism by itself is not enough.

3. Pay attention to your vocabulary. What words are coming out of your mouth, and what images are they portraying — positive and upbeat, or negative and cynical?

4. Engage in physical activity. A change in your physical self will help make a change in your emotional self.

5. Listen to lively music. It will help you feel more active.

6. Visualize the goals you set for yourself. With a realistic assessment of where you are now and a goal of where you want to go, you are on your way!

7. If you don't feel optimistic even though you know you should, fake it till you make it. Tell yourself the truth in advance.

8. Tell someone who is supportive of you about the changes you are trying to make. This leads to increased accountability.

9. Write things down. Write down the changes you think you have to make and keep a record of the progress you are making.

10. Help someone else who may need a lift to get out of his or her rut. There is a saying that, if you want to really understand something, teach it to someone else.

Being Content with Who and Where You Are

We have all seen folks who seem to have it all together, while others seem to have none of it together. Trying to understand the differences between the two is quite compelling. Contentment is a sense of satisfaction with who we are and what we do. The theme of this book has been how to move from where we are to where we want to be more quickly and easily. My experience and research suggests that there may be some common-thread conditions under which we find ourselves being most content, happiest, most satisfied and at peace. Many times we are most content:

When things fit. Ever had a pair of shoes that don't fit? What do we get? Blisters. Emotional blisters are even more uncomfortable. - We are most at peace when our lives reflect both our goals and values.

When we feel confident. We feel best when we are "good" at something, when we know what needs to be done and we do it.

When we feel connected. We are at our best when we feel connected to someone or something!

When we feel in control. We feel best when we feel at least somewhat in control of ourselves and our situations.

When we are autonomous. Another key to contentment is when we feel as though we are standing on our own two feet - when we are independent, not overly dependent on others or on things that we cannot control.

When we are communicating well. We are at our best when we are communicating well with others, but even more so when we have a high quality of internal dialogue.

When we are growing. We are best when we are looking forward, not back, when we are growing, not contracting.

When we are accepting. Things go more easily when we cut ourselves and others slack. When mistakes happen, don't dwell on them; instead, work to make the situation better.

When we are present, showing up even when we're not inclined. Procrastination is epidemic: Before you know it, "one of these days" turns into none of these days.

When we have come through a difficult challenge. Certainly, a sense of contentment doesn't often come while we are exerting all the effort to meet a challenge, but it does come sometime after. When we have put in the "full day," we can smile.

In Charge of Ourselves

Successful people recognize that they have control and choice over a number of key factors. Many of those key factors reside, not surprisingly, within ourselves:

Choose not to lose.   Whether we choose to focus on our problems or our possibilities is a key leadership issue. When faced with obstacles and failure, those who can overcome adversity and learn from their experiences, turning them into opportunities, are the ones who will be truly successful.

Choose your perceived reality.   Most so-called "facts" are open to interpretation and are highly dependent upon what's being read into them. We don't see the world as it is; we see it as we are. Too often, we let our problems trap us deep inside our own "reality rut." As long as we are stuck there, we can't see out of the rut to the possibilities beyond.

Choose an outlook.   An optimist expects the best possible outcome and concentrates on the most hopeful aspects of a situation.   Pessimists stress the negative and take the gloomiest possible view. While we may have been given a tendency toward optimism or pessimism at birth or from our upbringing, we can decide what we want to be from today forward.

Choosing to let go of deadly emotions.   Another painful, but liberating, milestone in our growth is when we accept responsibility for our emotions. It's less painful to believe that anger, jealousy or bitterness are somebody else's fault or beyond our control. Yet that only makes us prisoners of our emotions.   For our own health and happiness, we must exercise our choice to let go. No matter how long we nurse a grudge, it won't get better. We need to truly forgive and forget, because it lightens our emotional load.

Choose our thoughts. If we continue to think as we always have thought, we'll continue to get what we have always received. Our daily thought/choices translate into our daily actions. Our actions accumulate to form our habits. Our habits form our character. Our character attracts our circumstances. Our circumstances determine our future. Taking responsibility for our choices starts with choosing our thoughts.

Successful individuals realize that life accumulates; the choices we make, good and bad, are like deposits in a bank account.

Over the years, we can build up a wealth of success and happiness or a deficit of despair and discouragement. It's up to us. As with any active bank account, few of these choices are permanent. However, the longer we allow poor choices to accumulate, the more time and effort will be needed to undo them. Now is the time for action. There is still time. If not now, when?

Index

About the Author

Christopher is happily married to Kristin and has two children: Alexa Cate and Ryan Christopher. He has a BA from Rutgers University in History as well as a M.Ed. and Ed.D. from the University of Houston in Education. Christopher has taught in the Houston public school system as well as having taught at the collegiate level in New Hampshire and Pennslyvania. Currently Christopher teaches at Mount Union College in Alliance, Ohio.

Highly participative and animated, filled with energy, inspiration and fun, Chris' seminars put you and your group in the game, not sitting on the sidelines watching. There is no more powerful way to learn than by doing. By the end of your time together you will have had time to think and act. Christopher's passion is inspiring others to find their optimum level of performance and helping them find their personal level of success.

Christopher is available for keynote presentations, half day or one day seminars for businesses, executive retreats and association meetings. All of Christopher's seminars are customized for each individual audience.

Call **610-216-3575** to schedule an event for your group, or visit **http://www.christophersaffici.com**